More Praise for *Brave Church*

Hagan, out of her own difficult personal experiences and with a pastor's heart, calls us to create brave spaces—places of dialogue, challenge, grace, learning, and respect. In other words, she beckons us to be the church, nurturing communities of care as we engage our very lives. With her guidance, we can talk about tough topics!

—**Tyler Mayfield**, seminary professor and author of
A Guide to Bible Basics and *Unto Us a Child Is Born*

How is it that the church has been a place where the truth is suppressed instead of beckoned to be told? Too often, church folk choose to walk away from a disagreement or a faith community altogether instead of creating space where differences and truth-telling can coexist. If you're tired of the silence or the division, this book is for you. Hagan not only speaks her truth but also provides a roadmap for how pastors and laypeople can create critical truth-telling space that could be the key to setting people free.

—**Donna Claycomb Sokol**
Pastor, Mount Vernon Place United Methodist Church
Washington, DC

Hagan invites us to create accessible, brave, and vulnerable spaces in our churches—places where we can engage in tough talk about real life. With empathy and relatability, *Brave Church* urges Christians to think deeply, act boldly, and love unconditionally. Let's talk.

—**J. Dana Trent**, author of *Saffron Cross: The Unlikely Story of
How a Christian Minister Married a Hindu Monk*

If the list of topics covered in this book makes it feel too hot to handle, that's proof of how badly we need it. Winsomely written, well-researched, and eminently practical, this book is a gift to anyone who knows that a faithful church needs to tackle tough topics and longs for wise guidance on how.

—**L. Roger Owens**, Associate Professor of
Christian Spirituality and Ministry,
Pittsburgh Theological Seminary

In *Brave Church*, Hagan strives to integrate a divided church by bringing back the virtues of courage and truth and by calling the church to return to its highest ideals as a community of people willing to engage in honest conversations about the most difficult topics that challenge our theological assumptions and require us to wrestle with the pain and loss of our neighbors. Hagan tackles tough subjects the church has often avoided and offers real-life examples of communities striving to create brave space. *Brave Church* equips pastors and lay leaders with the tools and practices needed to invite their congregations into healthy and transformative dialogue. Those who accept the call of *Brave Church* will not only find the resources to cultivate courage and truth but also discover a path to deeper empathy and love, as well as the opportunity to help their church to become the most honest place in town.

—**W. Benjamin Boswell**, Senior Minister,
Myers Park Baptist Church
Charlotte, North Carolina

Elizabeth Hagan is brave, and *Brave Church* inspires me to be brave too. So many of us desire a richer, more honest, more relevant church, but we aren't sure how to get there. Whether you're a church leader yourself or you're a Christian who's frustrated with the church's inability to have hard conversations, *Brave Church* will give you hope and the necessary tools to move from stagnant inertia into honest conversations and transformational change.

—**Angela Denker**, Lutheran pastor
Author of *Red State Christians:*
Understanding the Voters Who Elected Donald Trump

BRAVE CHURCH

TACKLING TOUGH TOPICS
TOGETHER

ELIZABETH HAGAN

UPPER ROOM BOOKS®
NASHVILLE

Cover design: Molly von Borstel, Faceout Studio
Typesetting and interior design: PerfecType, Nashville, TN

Library of Congress Cataloging-in-Publication Data

Names: Hagan, Elizabeth, author.
Title: Brave church : tackling tough topics together / Elizabeth Hagan.
Description: Nashville, TN : Upper Room Books, 2020. | Includes
  bibliographical references. |
Identifiers: LCCN 2020001873 (print) | LCCN 2020001874 (ebook) | ISBN
  9780835819367 (paperback) | ISBN 9780835819374 (mobi) | ISBN
  9780835819381 (epub)
Subjects: LCSH: Church and social problems. | Interpersonal communication.
  | Social ethics—Religious aspects aspects—Christianity.
Classification: LCC HN31 .H24 2020 (print) | LCC HN31 (ebook) | DDC
  261.8/3—dc23
LC record available at https://lccn.loc.gov/2020001873
LC ebook record available at https://lccn.loc.gov/2020001874

Printed in the United States of America

For Beth,
who has taught me the joy of diligent study and
who abides with me in tough conversations

CONTENTS

ACKNOWLEDGMENTS

A book written for a community comes out of a community. My pastoral colleagues and social media friends helped direct me to many of the innovative ministries I explore in this book. I am thankful to each one of you who responded to my "please help!" emails and Facebook posts. You blessed me with your stories, your passion, and your desire to bring just a little more of the kingdom of heaven to earth. This book is stronger because you shared your words and time with me. I am grateful also to all the people who served as conversation partners as I dreamed about this book and who offered important feedback on the writing itself: Alice Stanton, Sarah Shelton, Glenda Elliott, Leslie Copeland-Tune, Carrie Zimmerman, Beth Dotson, J. Dana Trent, Abby Hailey, Kourtney Whitehead, Amanda Andere, Terry Magill, Amy Butler, Charlotte Rogers, Susan Smartt Cook, and Kevin Hagan.

The idea for this book came to me at the Wild Goose Festival in 2016 after my first meeting with Joanna Bradley Kennedy, who later brought this book to print with Upper Room Books. Joanna and the team at The Upper Room, thanks for believing in what I could offer. I'm so glad to be your partner in ministry. Thank you, Rachel Crumpler, for helping me to birth a more beautiful book with your thoughtful and kind editing. I am indebted also to the parishioners of Palisades Community Church in Washington, DC, who shaped many of the ideas presented in these pages. With your graciousness, I taught you as I wrote and leaned heavily on your feedback as I edited. With the confidence you gave me that discussions like this matter, I stayed the course. You are wise and kind people. Thank you for allowing me to be your pastor. Most of all I want to say thank you to my family who didn't grumble when I started writing again. Kevin, Amelia, and Sherlyne—your love and support ground me in my forever home. And I wrote this book with you in my heart, Landon.

INTRODUCTION

I grew up in a church that never felt real. In the suburban Tennessee church of my childhood, we talked about God, Jesus, and the Bible. We talked about Christmas pageants, bake sales, and chili suppers. We talked about outreach campaigns, volunteer missions, and Sunday school. But we never talked about real life. We never talked about the parts of life that made us sad, scared, angry, or ashamed. The father who went to jail on domestic assault charges later reappeared in church as if nothing happened. The woman who joyfully announced a pregnancy didn't say a word when her baby died in utero. The teen who attempted suicide returned to youth group, and the youth minister offered no lessons on living with depression. What happened outside of church walls stayed outside of polite church conversation, especially if it might make people uncomfortable. We kept our exchanges light and casual. We smiled. We put away our struggles when we pulled out our Bibles. We checked our heartaches and our messy, complicated lives at the church door.

I became a pastor because I wanted to be a part of a brave community. When asked to explain to seminary admission staff why I wanted to study theology, I could only say that I believed that there was another way of doing church than the way I knew. I believed that Jesus cared about my worst moments as much as he did my best. I believed that Jesus loved me in my mistakes and in my confusion. I was tired of all the fake smiling and shallow conversation. I was tired of hiding my painful experiences and sitting in silence when I disagreed with a majority opinion. I became a pastor because I wanted church to be authentic. I wanted church to be a place of unconditional welcome.

During the fifteen years I've served churches as a pastor, I've found how difficult it is to live out this mission. Being real with one another requires vulnerability, and some conversations don't feel safe in a public setting. Even if we are committed to being completely honest with one another, our church traditions do not support this open-hearted living. We have these unspoken rules about what we can and cannot share in church. In *Denial Is My Spiritual Practice*, Rachel G. Hackenberg recalls her church's traditions: "In worship it was acceptable to ask for prayers related to illness or death, but there were no prayer requests about suicide or sexuality, marital or financial problems. If they were said aloud at all, it was in private to the pastor, or the pastor's wife, or your dearest church friend."[1] These rules are hard to break; we might muster up the courage to whisper about our troubles in the hallway, but the idea of bringing them into the light of the sanctuary remains unthinkable. After years of looking past one another in the pews, looking one another in the eyes for the first time can feel like a weight we don't want to carry.

I chose to embrace vulnerability when I published a book about my struggle with infertility.[2] Bright-eyed and eager (and maybe naïve), I bravely offered my story. I figured that I could accept the discomfort of sharing the private details of my reproductive longings and failures. There's some distance, of course, between an author and her readers. I had forgotten that publishing a book comes with personal promotion and speaking engagements. I soon realized that on any given Sunday or Wednesday night I would have to stand before a congregation and utter phrases, like "periods that came late," "unprotected sex," and "pelvic ultrasounds." But I reminded myself that honesty and openness make us all feel less alone.

As I began to schedule these speaking engagements, I experienced firsthand the silencing power of church tradition. I never imagined how hard it would be to break the rules. Church leaders I had previously perceived as opened-minded would seek to censor my topic. For example, when I confirmed a promotional event with one church, I received an email that began this way: "Please do not plan to talk about infertility at the Wednesday event. Could you talk about a more general topic, like grief?" I wrote back right away: "Why? I wrote a book about infertility. That's my topic. You knew that when you invited me." Statistics show one in eight couples struggles to get and stay pregnant every year. Surely the church would welcome a conversation about this topic relevant to so many people. But, time and time again, I heard, "You can't talk about *that* here."

We can't talk about a lot of topics in church, I learned. Finding a solution to my marketing problems, I started leading workshops about grief. I invited people to extend their understanding of grief beyond mourning the death of a loved one. I spoke openly about the grief I experienced with infertility, and, in response, church members shared stories they might not have otherwise felt comfortable bringing into the sanctuary. As I facilitated workshops across the country, I heard real stories about infertility, miscarriage, addiction, mental illness, incarceration, infidelity, and singleness—all taboo topics in church.

Here's what else I learned: Our refusal to talk about tough topics can push people away from the church. During these grief workshops, I heard stories of Christians who felt silenced by their churches and who wondered if they still belonged. One woman who I will call Donna approached me after one workshop and offered her story: "Every time I bring it up to my pastor, he says we can't talk. I'm the faithful of the faithful," she said about her lifelong membership at a non-denominational church. "But I'm not sure I can go back anytime soon." She explained that her son recently had come out as gay. She told me that she did not approve of same-sex relationships; but she hoped the church that raised her son would continue to be a safe place for him as a young adult. Donna wanted to talk with someone about her frustrations and her theological questions. Donna wanted to speak up at church. "But I can't," she said.

Our churches often avoid topics that might be controversial. Yet, the Jesus I have grown to know and to love is the Jesus who was not scared of conflict. Jesus broke the rules when he asked the Samaritan woman for a drink at the well (see John 4:1-26). He paid no mind to the gossip when he shared a meal with a tax collector (see Luke 19:1-10).

He did not remain silent when the Pharisees introduced the woman caught in the act of adultery; neither did he condemn her (see John 8:1-11). As we follow the example that Jesus has set, we learn how to enter more bravely into these sometimes uncomfortable or even contentious conversations. We learn how to love and to wholly embrace people and all the stories they carry.

How do we make our churches places of unconditional welcome? How do we start talking about these tough topics—infertility and miscarriage, mental illness, domestic violence, racism, and sexuality? Holding in mind Donna's story and others I had been offered, I started writing. I wanted to create a resource that would help to facilitate these tough conversations in faith communities, that would help people to start talking. I wanted Donna and all the other people who had bravely shared their experiences with me to know that Jesus embraced people—all people—even in the messy, painful parts of their lives. The book you hold in your hands is that resource. The ultimate goal of this study is conversation—to talk about real life in your church. Our souls crave this connection. Even if your voice falters or the conversation gets uncomfortable, talking equals success. The next few pages will help you to get started.

GETTING STARTED

1. **Gather a small group.** Six to eight people is ideal. When I wrote this book, I envisioned you and some friends from church tackling these tough topics together in living rooms, around kitchen tables, or in church social halls. Do what works for your group. You might start your discussions with a meal as table fellowship can prepare relationships for growth. Even if you read this book on your own, jot down answers to the questions at the end of each chapter and then strike up a conversation with a couple of friends. You'll gain insight from listening to how other people think about these ideas.

2. **Include people with different perspectives.** Remember that the purpose of these conversations is not to sway others to a particular

ideological or theological position. While I hold my own beliefs about each topic, I wrote this book seeking to offer the highest respect to those members of our Christian family who hold beliefs that are different from my own. I hope that you will extend the same respect to each member of your group. (The first chapter will help you set some guidelines.) These conversations are not about right or wrong; they are about sharing stories with one another. By listening to other people's perspectives, we can experience God in new ways.

3. **Give every group member an opportunity to contribute to the conversation.** Try not to monopolize the microphone. If you are more outspoken and find yourself talking a lot in a conversation, consider not answering a question and allowing a quieter voice to be heard. This guideline is particularly important for group leaders. This study is not an opportunity for you to wax poetically about your thoughts on a topic. As a pastor, I believe that my work is accomplished when people talk and listen to one another with intention. Likewise, leaders, your job is not to lecture but to facilitate meaningful dialogue. Your job is to continually invite new perspectives into the conversation.

4. **Make room for reflection.** Remember that breakthroughs can happen when we are quiet. Though the goal of this study is to start talking, these conversations should not be rushed. Sometimes people need a minute to turn an idea over in their minds before they speak. Or people may need time to work up the courage to talk about a more personal experience. Instead of asking a new question to fill a lull, leaders observe the pause and wait another thirty seconds. If you lean into the silence, you might be surprised by the insights that arise.

HOW TO USE THIS BOOK

This book provides you with the framework and tools you need to have meaningful dialogue about tough topics. A leader's guide is included at the back of the book as well. Chapter 1 will guide your group in creating a covenant that can support you during tough conversations. The following five chapters introduce these topics: infertility and miscarriage (chapter 2); mental illness (chapter 3); domestic violence (chapter 4); racism (chapter 5); and sexuality (chapter 6). I organized these topics in order of difficulty based on my experience of facilitating these conversations. I started with topics that I thought would be easier entry points and ended with the more challenging and potentially controversial topics. I recognize, however, that what might be difficult for me or for my congregation might not be for you. Please feel free to talk about these topics in the order that works best for your church. As you conclude your study, chapter 7 offers space for reflection and for planning ways you can continue the conversations you have started.

Each chapter begins with scripture and a prayer that can ground your group before you begin your conversation. This spiritual grounding is vital. As Henri J. M. Nouwen, Catholic priest and spiritual teacher, tells us, "The deeper our communion with God is, the more we will discover [God] in all that we see."[3] The selected scripture and prayer serve as an introduction to the new topic; they also act as an invitation to stay in communion with God as you listen both to yourself and to others. Anyone in the group can read the scripture aloud and lead the group in prayer. After the prayer, each chapter is divided into the following sections:

Brave Exploration: This section presents current research and real stories that connect to the chapter's topic. It also explores how the topic intersects with church beliefs and traditions.

Brave Church: This section features churches (and a few nonprofit organizations) that have found ways to address the chapter's topic. These examples are intended to inspire you.

Brave Talk: Each chapter includes a list of reflection questions. These questions can help you to process the information you have received and provide a starting point for conversation.

Brave Act: This last section is a call to action. It offers a practical way for you to move forward—either by deepening your exploration of a topic or through an act of service.

I'm so glad you are here. I hope that, as you listen to the stories of your community, you see God in new ways. I hope that, as you bravely share your stories with one another, you experience the deep and abiding love of Christ. And I hope that, as a result of your time together, people will soon say about your church, "They talk about real life here."

CHAPTER 1

Let's Talk

Now there were staying in Jerusalem God-fearing Jews from every nation under heaven. When they heard this sound, a crowd came together in bewilderment, because each one heard their own language being spoken. Utterly amazed, they asked: "Aren't all these who are speaking Galileans? Then how is it that each of us hears them in our native language?"

—ACTS 2:5-8, NIV

The disciples gathered in the upper room and locked the door. They were lost, grieving, and afraid of what the future might hold. But something beautiful happened on Pentecost. The Spirit of God drew near, and a group of disciple-makers came to life. On the streets, people of all nationalities crowded "together in bewilderment" because they suddenly could understand one another. The winds and fire of the Spirit allowed people to truly see—heart to heart, soul to soul—and forever changed what is possible for human relationships. The story of Pentecost in Acts 2:1-12 invites us into community with people who hold opposing perspectives or who speak in a language we don't comprehend. The passage gives us hope that we can see, understand, and abide with one another.

With the blessing of the Spirit, we prepare for these tough conversations. The aim of this study is to start talking about real life together and to open ourselves to new ways of seeing God's work in our lives and in the lives of our neighbors. This chapter invites us to consider *how* this might be possible, how we might hear, understand and abide with one another, even during uncomfortable or contentious conversations. How can we create a community that is open to the Spirit of God, an environment that brings us "together in bewilderment"? To help us answer that question, this chapter begins with an exploration of environments that can foster (or stifle) meaningful dialogue. Then it offers some ground rules for groups to adopt for this study. These rules can form a covenant that supports each group member during hard conversations and allows us to learn and grow from one another's experiences.

As you gather your group for the first time, take a few moments to breathe. Breathe in. Breathe out. Know that the Spirit of God is with you. You are not alone. You've never been alone. God is with you. Begin by reading the scripture passage at the start of this chapter. Then, invite each person in the group to name an intention for the time you will spend together that answers this question: *What is your hope for the group as this study begins?* Then, ask one group member to read aloud this prayer:

> *Holy Spirit, as we begin this journey together, may we cease to be annoyed that others are not what we wish they were, since none of us is what we wish we were. Even in conflict, may we see people not as problematic but as beloved. Amen.*[1]

BRAVE EXPLORATION

One of the first places many of us feel the tension of human difference is within our families. While our family members may speak the same language, their perspectives can feel completely foreign. If your family is anything like mine, holiday gatherings are governed by unspoken rules. "Keep the peace" is one of the rules in my family. If your aunt's political campaigning offends your understanding of government, just nod and smile. Keep the peace. If your grandfather's choice of language about other racial groups feels wrong, stay quiet. Keep the peace. If the presence of your cousin's husband of the same sex makes you uncomfortable, say nothing. Keep the peace. As a child, I always wondered why. Was conflict wrong?

When I began serving congregations as a pastor, I learned quickly that my family wasn't unique. Families adopt all sorts of silencing behaviors. In my first parish, I remember the Sunday after Thanksgiving when this twentysomething collapsed on the couch in my office. Between sniffles, Jana told me about the terrible time she'd had at home during the holiday. Her family never spoke about Uncle Mike's heavy drinking. Maybe it was not her place to do so, she mused, but she couldn't help herself. Tension pushed Jana to confront her uncle. She asked Mike not to open another bottle of tequila. Jana's mom (Mike's sister) stood silent as he erupted in rage. Mike called Jana names that she didn't want to repeat in my office and then chased her out of the condo. "I can't imagine going home at Christmas now," she sobbed. "My family is no longer safe." Sometimes we remain silent to keep the peace and, sadly, sometimes because we are afraid of harm.

Safe Spaces

Jana needed a place to share this story. She needed a safe space—a place protected from the threat of verbal abuse or physical harm—to process her thoughts and feelings about the experience. For Jana on that Sunday afternoon, my office offered such refuge. In my office, Jana could retreat from the distress she felt with her family at that moment. She could find comfort in knowing that I would listen to her viewpoints without judgment and that I would accept her unconditionally. Safe spaces provide emotional and spiritual support for people who feel their values, identity, or expressed boundaries have been violated in some way. Even without naming particular spaces "safe," many of us have found them: the chair in our therapist's office, the kitchen table at our beloved aunt's home, or our best friend's back patio. Safe spaces offer understanding, comfort, and belonging—gifts our souls crave in a world of so much division. We all need safe spaces, but these spaces are of particular importance to marginalized populations. Consider this scenario: Let's say you are traveling abroad in a country where English is not readily spoken. After days of frustrating exchanges, imagine your delight at running into fellow travelers who share your native tongue. Imagine what a relief it would be to relax into easy conversation. Safe spaces can offer the same relief to groups of people that are underrepresented or marginalized in our communities. For people who experience discrimination due to their nationality, race, ethnicity, gender, or sexual orientation, safe spaces provide a place to relax. This is why my friend Mila, originally from Guatemala, joined a salsa club and why my friend Katherine has coffee every week with the Women's Business Alliance. In these safe spaces, gatherings of like-minded people, they can freely be themselves.

Now common vernacular, the phrase *safe space* came into use in the mid-1900s. Colleges and universities picked up the phrase and institutionalized the concept in the 1990s and 2000s. Many schools today still designate and protect safe spaces for campus groups like the Latino Alliance, Military and Veteran Student Center, LBGTQ Student Alliance, Sexual Assault Center, Women's Center, and African American Student Union. With special training, faculty and staff can mark their offices as safe spaces—places where students can seek support in moments of crisis and know that they will be welcomed without judgment.[2] As a student at Duke Divinity School in 2003, I sought out a professor with an "I'm safe" sticker on her door. I was being harassed by another student, and after receiving many threatening phone calls, I feared what might happen if he showed up unannounced at my home. This professor connected me with the campus resources I needed to continue my studies. I don't know how I would have stayed in school during that difficult semester without the support I received in that safe space.

Safe spaces (institutional sites of support as well as informal gatherings of like-minded people) can be a huge benefit to our mental, emotional, and spiritual health. But there is a time for everything. It is all too easy to sink into the safety of the familiar, like a comfortable couch, and not want to leave the reassurance of friendly voices and the ideas that support our own. This is the drawback of safe spaces: We begin to expect people to unconditionally accept our beliefs. We forget how to listen to new perspectives. We forget how to learn from challenges. Keeping us close to like-minded people, safe spaces can rob us of the opportunity to build community with people who see the world differently than we do. But how do we venture beyond these comfortable places of understanding and acceptance? Many of us don't know where to start.

"From Safe Spaces to Brave Spaces"

Several years ago, I was delighted to discover an alternative to safe spaces presented in the work of student affairs educators Brian Arao and Kristi Clemens. Facilitating diversity trainings at New York University, the two educators made this observation: In safe spaces, conversations about tough topics, like racial equity, often resulted in stalemate. Students avoided difficult subjects, skirted challenges, and talked over one another. No one listened, and the conversations stopped. Arao and Clemens believed there had to be a better way. While maintaining the importance of safe spaces on campus, the educators wondered if there might be a better environment for their diversity trainings, one that allowed participants to listen to one another and to learn from challenges.

In their groundbreaking 2013 case study, "From Safe Spaces to Brave Spaces," published in *The Art of Effective Facilitation*, the educators suggest that brave space might be the ideal environment for hard conversations. Talking about tough topics, Arao and Clemens observed, "often requires the very qualities of risk, difficulty, and controversy that are defined as incompatible with safety."[3] They asked the students to try a new environment, to shift from the expectations of safe spaces to those of brave spaces; the change allowed students to adopt new intentions for conversation. In brave spaces, Arao and Clemens observed, group members made space for differing viewpoints and listened to previously silenced voices. Hard conversations require courage—the courage to listen and to learn, the courage to challenge viewpoints and to admit wrongdoing. The conversations that occur in brave spaces may be uncomfortable, but they allow us to build stronger communities.

In their work, Arao and Clemens give us the tools we need to venture out of our comfortable safe spaces. The educators look first at five common rules (spoken or unspoken) followed in safe spaces; they explain how these rules can limit conversations by confining participants to only comfortable topics or by discouraging the risks necessary for learning and growth. Arao and Clemens then propose a new set of rules for the establishment of brave spaces:

1. **Controversy with civility**: Accept controversial opinions and conflict.
2. **Own your intentions and your impact**: Know your words can hurt other people.
3. **Challenge by choice**: Step in and out of tough conversations freely.
4. **Respect**: Find out what respect means to different people.
5. **No personal attacks**: Challenge ideas, not people.[4]

These rules, the educators believe, will encourage the risk-taking necessary for engaging in hard conversations. Brave spaces allow people to talk about tough topics, to stay in conversation with one another, and to gain insight they might not have ever had if they stayed in safe spaces alone.

Moving Toward a Brave Church

As I read Arao and Clemens's discussion of safe spaces and brave spaces, my mind immediately went to the church. I thought about how churches are designed to be safe spaces—places we can worship without fear of persecution. We seek out churches as a way to connect with people who hold similar convictions about God, the Bible, death, and resurrection. In church, we do not have to explain or defend our faith to nonbelievers. Many Christians add another layer of support by worshiping in congregations of similar race, socioeconomic status, or country of origin. One church I pastored in Maryland shared its building with two congregations, one Burmese and one Brazilian. While many members spoke English and could have attended our main worship service, they choose to gather separately. Their spiritual lives benefited from this time set apart to worship with other people who shared their native tongue and understood their cultural traditions. With whomever we choose to worship, Sunday service gives us a break from the stress and strain of the world. We hope to emerge from church with renewed strength, ready to return to the parts of our lives that may not be as welcoming to our Christian identity.

Embracing our churches as safe spaces, we receive the gifts of comfort, connection, and belonging. But maintaining safe space indefinitely can shut down conversations that we need to have. It can keep us from our Great Commission to go into the world and make disciples (see Matthew 28:19). It can cut us off from our neighbors that Jesus has called us to love (see Matthew 22:39). It can rob us of the opportunity to witness the Holy Spirit at work as we build community with people who see the world differently than we do. Following Jesus is never a stagnant journey. As Arao and Clemens point out in their work, we need safe spaces *and* brave spaces to grow and strengthen our communities. Their guidelines for brave spaces give us new tools for our journey. Using these guidelines, we can create an environment that allows us to start talking about real life, to stay in hard conversations, and to learn from one another. In a brave space, we can embrace the messiness of our human lives and support one another in authentic communities of faith. We can become brave churches alive with the power of Pentecost and unafraid of what new thing God might do among us.

BRAVE CHURCH

In the summer of 2019, I led a pilot study for my own brave church. I was a pastor in Washington, DC, where it is common for church members to have careers in government, to serve as political appointees, and to have deep connections to ideas that starkly divide them from their neighbors. I figured if our congregation could talk about the tough top-ics in this book, then any church could. For six weeks, we maintained a brave space for conversations about infertility and miscarriage, mental illness, domestic violence, racism, and sexuality. And, I tell you, every-one survived.

In this section, I share with you the covenant rules my congregation adopted for this study. (You can find the complete covenant in appen-dix A.) Our covenant is built on the rules for brave spaces that Arao and Clemens present in "From Safe Spaces to Brave Spaces." I heavily draw on their work as I offer a rationale for each rule in the pages that follow. While I believe this covenant will prepare you to talk about tough top-ics, I encourage you to shape it to support your specific needs. As you enter into covenant together, remember confidentiality is important for any sacred group. The time you spend together should be set apart from other conversations you have in your everyday life.

RULE 1: We will accept conflict and commit to the way of kindness.

Let's just agree to disagree. How many times have you heard a discussion ended this way? The phrase pops up at family dinners and in many pub-lic debates. My friend Carrie, a diversity and inclusivity consultant for universities, suggests what we mean is this: "I like you too much to fight with you" or "I don't want to talk about *that* anymore."[5] A common rule for safe spaces, agreeing to disagree ends conversations in our churches too. I recently encountered a church with a safe word that members could use when a conversation got too controversial. Brave spaces, in contrast, embrace conflict as a natural part of tough conversations. Arao and Clemens believe that examining sources of tension can strengthen diverse communities, so they suggest that we accept "controversy with civility."[6] This ground rule for brave spaces is of vital importance. If we want to have conversations about real life in church, we will experience moments of conflict and controversy. Repeat after me: *Not everyone in my church is going to agree with me, and that's OK.*

Brave churches accept conflict and commit to the way of kindness. We do not avoid or ignore controversial ideas. We do not respond to disagreements by ending the conversation. Nor do we approach conflict as a debate that can be won. We listen. We consider the tone of our voice, and we keep talking with one another. We remember that we are all children of God. Brave churches believe that we can share space with people with whom we disagree. Brave churches believe that by exploring the roots of our disagreement and staying in conversation, we can strengthen our community of faith.

RULE 2: We will take responsibility for how our own words are received.

Don't take things personally. This safe space mantra asks us to set aside our judgments and emotional responses. In tough conversations, the rule can encourage greater participation and honesty as it frees participants from the fear that they will be labeled (for example, sexist, racist, homophobic). For instance, when we are worried a comment will offend someone, we might say, "Now, don't take this the wrong way, but . . ." The phrase acts as a disclaimer, letting us off the hook for any hurt feelings or anger our words might cause. However, as Arao and Clemens point out, the phrase invalidates emotional responses and silences people who may be hurt. It also does a disservice to the speaker who remains unaware of the harm and unable to make amends. "Own your intentions and your impact," the educators urge us.[7] As social researcher Brené Brown writes, "Courage is forged in pain, but not in all pain. Pain that is denied or ignored becomes fear or hate."[8] Brave spaces make room for pain. When we listen to the pain our group members express and take responsibility for the harmful impact of our words, we deepen bonds of trust.

Brave churches recognize that words can cause harm, and we take responsibility for how our words are received. We recognize that we are all imperfect and that we may say sexist, racist, patriarchal, homophobic, or otherwise hurtful things. Brave churches know these mistakes do not make us bad people but rather people whose words have caused harm. During the pilot study, one group member recalled a time when she told a joke at a church board meeting. She was unaware of the joke's racial undertones; she didn't intend any harm. But when a friend took offense, she bravely took responsibility for her mistake. She apologized for the hurt it caused and promised to never tell the joke again. As theologian and author Barbara Brown Taylor writes, "Every human interaction offers you the chance to make things better or to make things worse."[9] When we hurt other people, intentionally or unintentionally, we have a chance to repair the damage. Brave churches humbly acknowledge mistakes and pledge to keep learning.

RULE 3: We will ask permission before we challenge someone's views on a subject.

When we embrace our churches wholly as safe spaces, we often come to believe that we should always be comfortable in church. When a controversial topic or uncomfortable subject emerges, we stay quiet. We keep the peace. When we don't have something nice to say at church, we hold our tongues out of respect for the comfort of others in the room. Yet maintaining that comfort comes with a price. It limits the conversations we are able to have. It silences voices of dissent and expressions of pain. It shuts down challenges that might lead to new growth.

Brave churches, in contrast, set aside comfort for the good of challenging the norm. We believe we can grow from challenges posed to our current ways of thinking. We believe engaging in these tough conversations can allow us to see God in new ways. But here is the key: To honor the boundaries of our group members, we ask permission before we challenge one another. We accept that some participants may not be up for a challenge in the moment. During the pilot study of this book, one group member asked another for permission to challenge him. When he agreed, she said, "I hear what you are saying. But have you thought about how your perspective is grounded in sexism?" The group member seemed taken aback; he had not intended to make a sexist remark. But his discomfort did not overwhelm his curiosity and desire to learn.

An honest and respectful exchange followed and then later continued over coffee. Exploring sources of conflict may be uncomfortable. Asking hard questions, of course, doesn't always lead to easy answers or simple solutions. Brave churches thrive in the tension.

RULE 4: We will show respect for one another and graciously receive feedback if someone feels disrespected.

Respect is a rule everyone can agree on. In safe spaces, group members might pledge to honor each person's point of view—a noble intention of humility. In brave spaces, Arao and Clemens invite us to consider what respect means to each group member. Respect, the educators found, means different things to different people; the way I demonstrate respect might be different than the way you do. Arao and Clemens encourage us to think concretely about our different expectations and even to practice ways we might respectfully challenge one another.[10]

A discussion about respect can give us new ways to care for one another and to understand the world. One group member in the pilot study shared how conversations with his daughter have pushed him to reconsider what respectful language looks like. For sixty years of his life, this participant has used exclusively the pronouns *she* or *he* to refer to another individual. He's learning now from his daughter and her friends that respectful language might include the pronoun *they*. Though habits of speech can be hard to break, he's trying to make the change in order to show respect for others who see the world differently.

Brave churches show respect to every member of the congregation. We begin by learning what respect means to each person. We ask each of our group members how they would like to be addressed. We find out what titles and pronouns they use for themselves and what casual forms of address make them most comfortable. As brave churches, we are willing to learn from one another and to reconsider the language we have used in the past. We are willing to change our habits in an effort to show respect to everyone in our community. We know that we may falter and agree to graciously receive feedback if our words have hurt someone in the group.

RULE 5: We will use "I" instead of "you" statements. We will not accuse or attack.

A rule safe spaces and brave spaces share is "no attacks"—no name-calling or hateful challenges to someone's identity. Brave spaces, however, welcome challenges to ideas. When a pointed challenge causes discomfort, Arao and Clemens observed, we sometimes perceive it as a personal attack and stop the conversation. The educators encourage us to distinguish between attacks and challenges: "Your idea is dumb" is an attack, but we might challenge by saying, "That idea makes me angry." When a challenge feels like an attack, the educators suggest we explore the cause of our discomfort and the roots of our defensive response.[11]

Brave churches engage in hard conversations with open minds and loving hearts. While we may disagree about these tough topics, we do not make personal attacks. We do not call people names or accuse one another. Brave churches do, however, challenge ideas. If I've received verbal consent (see rule 3), I can challenge your idea; I might tell you how I perceive your idea, how it makes me feel, or why I believe it needs further explanation. When we challenge ideas, we make "I" statements ("I feel . . .") rather than "you" statements ("You are . . ."). We ask earnest questions to make sure we hear and understand one another. Brave churches invite group members to critically examine their ideas and to consider new perspectives—not to declare one right and another wrong but to keep learning in community.

Becoming a Brave Church

My hope is that you will become a brave church—engaging in conversations about the tough topics in this study and beyond. Becoming a brave church is a journey. A covenant is a tool to guide you. As you embark on this journey, take time to make a covenant with your group members. (You can use the one provided in appendix A or create your own.) Remember that no one is perfect and that these rules may be broken from time to time. Keep talking with one another not only about the topics in this book but also about the environment you are creating and the experience you are sharing. Promise to help one another to become a braver and more loving congregation.

If you take up this challenge, please know you are doing no small thing. Most churches find their foundation as a safe space—if that. It requires an act of courage to step beyond the comfort we find in our shared Christian faith and to engage in hard conversations about real life. These conversations may open us to uncomfortable realities and challenge our assumptions about ourselves, others, and even our churches. For instance, one participant in the pilot study asked us to stop and consider the ways in which our church was *not* safe. Were we *really* welcoming to all, as we liked to boast? With the brave space rules, this participant could challenge these assumptions. In particular, this participant challenged our congregation to consider how someone with political affiliations underrepresented in our church might feel when parishioners requested prayers for certain congressional bills. From his challenging questions, I learned I can never assume that a faith community is a safe space for everyone. The conflict allowed our congregation to explore the ways we needed to change to better serve to our specific community and to become a more welcoming church for all.

Learning and growing is hard work! Know that these challenging conversations can drain you mentally and emotionally. Brave space discussions demand a lot from people, especially from those who do not share the dominant viewpoint. It can be exhausting to educate group members about a different perspective or to share a painful life experience. As a participant in the pilot study offered, you may want to retreat to the comfort of a safe space when the conversation ends. For her, that meant attending a support group meeting or going to a trusted friend's house. She encouraged other participants to identify what that space might be and to make plans ahead of time.

While the difficulties of this work should not be underestimated, these tough conversations are worth the effort. Talking about real life can transform our churches. As we learn to accept controversy, we can stop asking beloved children of God, "Whose team are you on?" As we learn to approach people with a holy curiosity, we start asking, "How do you experience God's presence in your life?" When we can really hear people's responses—even if the story they tell makes us uncomfortable or challenges us in some way—we live into our Pentecost identity.

BRAVE TALK

1. Reread Acts 2:1-12. What parts of the narrative stand out to you? What can this story teach you about your relationships? How might this scripture passage guide you during the next sessions of this study?
2. Describe a time when you felt wholly welcomed by a group of people. What gifts did you receive from this experience?
3. Describe a time when you felt afraid or unwelcome in a group of people. What made you feel unwelcome? How did you respond to that experience?
4. How does your current church function as a safe space (or not)? What qualities have made your church feel safe or unsafe to you?
5. What are some differences between safe spaces and brave spaces? What does it mean to become a brave church?

BRAVE ACT

Review the covenant found in appendix A. After you read and discuss each rule using the information provided in this chapter, you might explore these questions: Which rule(s) have you practiced in the past? Which rule(s) will be the most challenging for you? Are there rules you would like to add or edit? Feel free to modify the covenant to meet the needs of your group, keeping in mind what you've learned about safe spaces and brave spaces. As a final step, each person should sign the covenant as you commit to becoming a brave church together.

CHAPTER 2

Let's Talk About Infertility and Miscarriage

In her deep anguish Hannah prayed to the LORD, weeping bitterly. And she made a vow, saying, "LORD Almighty, if you will only look on your servant's misery and remember me, and not forget your servant but give her a son, then I will give him to the LORD for all the days of his life."
—1 SAMUEL 1:10-11, NIV

*H*ave you ever longed for something that you couldn't have or that seemed just out of your reach? For couples who want to have a baby, infertility and miscarriage can shatter any illusion of control. You cannot will yourself to conceive, of course. You can do everything "right," and still nothing happens. You may be unable to get pregnant, or you may be unable to carry a pregnancy to full term. Many couples who experience infertility and miscarriage will go on to birth babies or to welcome children into their families in other ways. However, the loss they have experienced stays forever imprinted on their hearts. Children who should have been are not.

We are introduced to a woman longing for a child in the First Book of Samuel. Hannah wants to have a baby, but "the LORD had closed her womb" (1 Sam. 1:5). In other words, no one knows why she can't conceive. Living with infertility, Hannah waits year after year as her friends, her relatives, and her husband's other wife announce pregnancies and deliver babies. Experiencing loss, isolation, and the pain of a future she can't control, Hannah wonders and wails: *Why didn't I get pregnant this month? Why can't I be like everyone else? Will I ever have a baby?* Her anguish leads her to take drastic measures. She enters the Temple praying and weeping, without considering who might hear her longings. She bargains with God, as many of us do in a moment of crisis. Hannah cries, "If you give me a son, I will offer him back to you." She prays with such fervor that Eli, the priest, thinks she is drunk! Though Hannah later conceives, her journey to motherhood speaks of the deep pain of longing.

As you gather for conversation, begin with a moment of reflection. Think about a time that you were praying for something that you really, really wanted and that just wasn't coming. Share a word or phrase that describes that unfulfilled longing. Then, ask one group member to read aloud this invocation:

> *God, we gather today not to run from pain but to come close to it. Give us the courage to offer our unfinished stories without sugarcoating them. Challenge us to see beyond our own experiences. Offer us peace for our wounds of loss that have not yet healed, and help us to be gentle with one another. Amen.*

BRAVE EXPLORATION

We rarely hear the words *infertility* or *miscarriage* spoken aloud in a congregational setting, let alone by a pastor in the pulpit. Yet, statistics tell us that these concerns are quite common. Infertility affects one in eight couples in the United States.[1] Between 10–15 percent of confirmed pregnancies (roughly one in eight) end in miscarriage.[2] This percentage would be higher if it included the loss of unconfirmed pregnancies; many miscarriages occur before eight weeks into pregnancy, often too early to be counted as "real" by the medical community. But these losses still weigh heavily on parents' hearts. If infertility or miscarriage has not been a part of your family's story, you probably know many people who have experienced these struggles, even if they haven't told you about it.

This story belongs to both men and women; the inability to get pregnant can be caused by male infertility (30 percent), female infertility (30 percent), or a combination of the two.[3] However, this chapter focuses on women's experience of infertility and miscarriage. Women who struggle with infertility hold the pain of unfulfilled longing but also the shame of not living up to social expectations. In *You're Doing It Wrong! Mothering, Media, and Medical Expertise*, researchers Bethany L. Johnson and Margaret M. Quinlan explain, "The inability to conceive is still problematically framed as a female failure in a society where female value is linked to reproduction and women are assumed to be 'natural mothers.'"[4] Women carry babies in their bodies. Women also carry the pain of children not coming from their bodies.

Stories of Infertility and Miscarriage

Of all the tough topics explored in this book, this one has most significantly impacted my life. At the age of twenty-eight, one year into marriage and one year into my first solo pastorate, my husband and I started trying to conceive. My body was healthy. My heart felt ready. With my get-things-done approach to life, I knew I would be announcing a pregnancy in no time. I knew, as much as I'd felt called to the pastorate, God also called me to motherhood. But I did not expect, in pursuit of this calling, I would experience three miscarriages, nine infertility treatments, including six rounds of in vitro fertilization (IVF), and two failed adoptions. After eight years of longing for a baby, my husband and I became parents through a successful adoption in 2016.

During those long eight years, like Hannah, I prayed and I wailed. But, unlike Hannah, I never became pregnant. I was overwhelmed by the loss, the longing, and the persistent feeling that God had somehow forgotten me. I often collapsed, unable to carry out basic life tasks. Despair brought new stress into my work, my friendships, and my marriage. My husband and I sometimes wondered if our relationship would withstand the strain. And throughout this season of my life, I felt like I couldn't talk openly about my experience, especially not at church—the place where I spent most of my time.

I hid my pain from the congregation I served. I remember leading a baby dedication for a congregant one Sunday. I recently had experienced a miscarriage, but I somehow pulled myself together for worship. I held the new baby, blessing her and walking her around the sanctuary. I looked at her tiny fingers and toes as I breathed in the smell of baby lotion. It took every ounce of my energy not to cry. Then, over coffee after the service, a well-meaning parishioner cooed, "How natural you look with a baby!" Another asked, "When are you going to have one?" An elderly lady exclaimed, "I'm so glad we finally have a pastor who's still menstruating!" How could I break the news to them that, menstruating or not, I wasn't sure I could ever contribute to the nursery quota? I felt like a failure. I wanted to be a mother, but my body had betrayed me. I could not do the thing that I wanted to do and that so many people wanted me to experience too.

My experience was not uncommon. After publishing a memoir, *Birthed: Finding Grace Through Infertility,* I spoke with congregations across the country and met many couples struggling to conceive or carry a pregnancy to full term.[5] I learned that infertility and miscarriage can drive even the most outgoing people into silence. Who wants to talk about their sex life publicly—especially at church? Infertility is a stew of "sexuality, shame, anger, body image issues, and envy," as a woman in my workshop put it. "Now who would want to order that?" So we don't talk about infertility. Rather than forcing uncomfortable conversations, we smile, we make small talk, and we bury our pain. The secrecy and shame of infertility and miscarriage leads to isolation and, for many women like me, depression.

Churches inadvertently deepen those feelings of isolation when they center fellowship opportunities for young couples on the common bonds of parenthood. A lifelong Christian in her thirties, whom I'll call Renee, started worshiping at an Episcopal church shortly after she and her husband moved to a Midwest town. When Renee began seeking consultation and treatment for infertility, she shared this information with some friends she had made through work. But she didn't talk about the ups and downs of infertility at church. "The people our age hung out in the hallway where the nursery and the kid's Sunday school classes were," Renee explained. "We, of course, had no reason to go down that hall, so we didn't know how to mingle." She spoke favorably of the church, noting the warm welcome she and her husband received in the sanctuary. After the service, however, they became keenly aware of "being on the outside of something we deeply wanted." Renee wanted to be in the parent club, and going to church felt like a reminder of how she didn't belong.

Infertility and miscarriage affect not only women in their thirties, like Renee, but women of all ages. And these struggles can bring a lifetime of pain. After a workshop I led in a church in North Carolina, a woman in her early sixties approached me. With grandkids hanging on her hips, she was the person I least expected to be interested in my presentation. Yet, she told me how she and her husband conceived their daughter via IVF in the late 1980s when no one talked about IVF. I asked if anyone at her church knew. "No, I've carried this secret for years." She described the shame and embarrassment she felt when she was not able to get or stay pregnant. "I still can remember how much I wanted a baby and prayed in church for one for all those years." Our longings for children can leave deep wounds.

Mother's Day and Father's Day Traditions in the Church

For those without children, the most damaging days of church life are Mother's Day and Father's Day. Cherry, a woman in her thirties who found out she suffered from infertility after a cancer diagnosis, told me that she dreads going to church on these holidays. "At our church," she said, "they go all out by selling flowers at the church for all of the parents, seemingly without noticing that there may be a few hopeful hearts with deferred dreams sitting in the pews."[6] While Mother's Day and Father's Day are not a part of the liturgical year, these holidays are celebrated often with the same gusto as Christmas or Easter. Many churches promote these Sundays with special banners and Facebook posts promising prizes for all the parents in attendance, special anthems about a mother's love, or cook-offs for fathers only. Many pastors preach about parenting and often ask the mothers and fathers to stand while the congregation claps. Non-mothers and non-fathers stay seated.

Other churches, wanting to be more inclusive, declare that Mother's Day honors all women and Father's Day all men. I was a guest preacher at one such church on Mother's Day. Every woman in attendance received a corsage prepared by the women's mission circle. How beautiful those flower arrangements looked! Yet, not every woman was pleased with the offering. I could see the discomfort on the faces of women without children. I overheard one woman say to a friend, "I just don't know why I was forced to take one of these. It's just weird. I'm not a mother." Not all women are mothers, and not all men are fathers. That is OK. These well-intentioned gestures of inclusivity can create awkward experiences for women and men who are not parents (for any number of reasons) and feel little connection to the holidays.

The History of Mother's Day and Father's Day

Digging into the history of these holidays, we learn that both Mother's Day and Father's Day were first celebrated in churches. The woman who created Mother's Day, Anna Jarvis, did not have any children of her own. She petitioned for the holiday as a way to honor her mother, Ann Reeves Jarvis. Ann birthed thirteen children, but she only saw four of them live beyond childhood. Her loss sparked a passion for advocacy. In her Appalachian community during the late-1800s, many infants died from diseases spread by poor sanitary conditions. During the typhoid fever epidemic, Ann Reeves Jarvis helped to organize local educational events that provided information about good hygiene practices. She called these events Mothers' Day Work Clubs.[7] Anna Jarvis was heartbroken when her mother died in 1905, and she wanted to honor her mother's commitment to helping others. She began petitioning politicians, writers, businessmen, and governors to designate the second Sunday in May (the Sunday closest to her mother's death) "Mother's Day." In 1908, Anna helped to organize the first Mother's Day celebration at Andrew Methodist Episcopal Church in Grafton, West Virginia. The state declared Mother's Day a holiday two years later; then in 1914, to honor mothers whose sons died in the war, President Woodrow Wilson made it a national holiday.[8]

While Father's Day took a little longer to catch on, this holiday also took root in church. In July 1908, a few months after the first Mother's Day celebration, the church now known as Central United Methodist Church held the first Father's Day service in Fairmont, West Virginia. The church organized the one-time event after an accident killed more than three hundred and fifty men in a nearby mine. At the suggestion of a parishioner, the pastor performed a Father's Day service inspired by Exodus 20:12 to honor of the men who had died and the children they had left behind.[9] A few years later in Spokane, Washington, Sonora Louise Smart Dodd organized another Father's Day event. After hearing a Mother's Day sermon, Dodd decided there should be a day that honored fathers too. Her own father, a Civil War veteran, single-handedly raised six children after the death of his second wife. Slowly states across the country began observing the holiday. Finally, in 1972, President Richard Nixon made Father's Day a national holiday.[10]

Suggestions for Sensitivity and Change

Knowing the history and founding spirit of Mother's Day and Father's Day, we are better equipped to examine how we celebrate these holidays in our churches today. Instead of insisting, as many churches do, "let's keep doing things the way we've always done them," let's reimagine these services in a way that reflects their original intent—to honor those who care for us. How might we uphold that intention while being sensitive to church members who do not have children by choice or by circumstance? I would like to offer a couple of suggestions:

- **Create a more inclusive worship plan for Mother's Day and Father's Day.** If you are on the church's leadership team, write liturgies that speak to the many ways we nurture children. (See appendix B.) Preach sermons about what it means for God to be a mother or father and how we can all be more like God in this way. Pray for the grieving. Speak to the pain of couples who are struggling with infertility or miscarriage. Be empathetic; imagine what it feels like for church members to be seen and heard on a holiday loaded with Hallmark expectations.

- **Serve your community.** Remember Ann Reeves Jarvis used the term "Mother's Day" to describe her outreach events. Ann, a Sunday school teacher, wanted to support other mothers in her community and to improve their quality of life. Are there parents who could use support in your community? Collect diapers for mothers caring for babies while experiencing homelessness. Donate to an organization that provides assistance to single parents. Shifting the focus from "honoring parents" to "helping parents in need" allows the whole congregation to take part.

As you consider how your church might be more sensitive to couples without children, remember that respect may look different to you than it does to other people. When you start preparing for Mother's Day and Father's Day, invite church members without children into the conversation. You might be surprised by what comes out of that collaboration.

BRAVE CHURCH

As you create a more welcoming environment for couples experiencing infertility, you may also want to make available educational resources and a list of faith-based infertility support groups. Many secular non-profit organizations, like RESOLVE, help women to form support groups and talk about their struggles; however, I've found that Christians crave guidance and support from other women who share their beliefs. In this section, you will find two faith-based nonprofits and one church providing that support.

Moms in the Making

Moms in the Making is a faith-based infertility support group that was founded by Caroline Harries in 2013. The nonprofit organization began as an in-person meetup in Dallas, Texas; women struggling with infertility would gather in Harries's living room to talk and pray for one another. When women receive an infertility diagnosis, they are presented with a range options, including fertility drugs, IVF, donor semen or eggs, surrogacy, adoption, etc. Trying to bring a baby into your family often means making a lot of tough choices and, in many cases, trying and trying and trying again. Moms in the Making helps women to navigate their options and offers a supportive environment for women to explore the spiritual and ethical implications of these decisions. Harries moved the group online in 2015, and by 2017, Moms in the Making boasted an annual conference and thousands of members. The online testimonies and the Facebook comments posted during monthly prayer nights can attest to the value of a Christian support group. Many women who feel isolated and who don't feel comfortable talking about infertility at church find community through this online network.[11]

Fertility for Colored Girls

Another nonprofit organization that supports women with infertility and has roots in the faith sector is Fertility for Colored Girls. Executive Minister at Trinity United Church of Christ in Chicago Rev. Dr. Stacey Edwards-Dunn started the nonprofit in 2013. It provides African American women with reproductive education and a space for conversations about infertility and miscarriage—support Edwards-Dunn wished she had during her own journey to motherhood. She and her husband tried for six years, including eight rounds of IVF, before welcoming their daughter in 2014. She recalls her surprise when she first learned that she was living with infertility. Although African American women are almost two times more likely to experience infertility than white women, Edwards-Dunn said that stereotypes perpetuate misinformation: "We are told that Black women aren't supposed to have these problems, that we are basically baby-making machines."[12] She remembers feeling ashamed of her infertility. She didn't talk about it with her friends, and she didn't talk about it with parishioners, not even those seeking her counseling for the same troubles.[13] Edwards-Dunn started Fertility for Colored Girls because she did not want other women to grieve and hope in silence. The nonprofit helps to combat problematic stereotypes, offers information about different paths to motherhood, provides grief support, and hosts websites for testimony and connection.[14]

Cornerstone Church in Grand Rapids, Michigan

Some churches have created their own support groups for women struggling with the grief of infertility and miscarriage. A trailblazing member of Cornerstone Church, Sarah Sisson Rollandini founded an infertility support group for her congregation. Rollandini longed for a child for ten years while enduring fertility treatments and miscarriage before building a family through gestational surrogacy and adoption. Motivated by 2 Corinthians 1:4, which calls us to comfort others as God comforts us, Rollandini wanted to encourage other women in her church. "I believe that every church should offer an infertility ministry or collaborate with other churches to offer a centralized ministry for couples struggling with infertility," Rollandini said.[15] A typical support group meeting at Cornerstone includes an icebreaker question, a book study, and a time for sharing goals and updates.

By creating new support groups or by connecting members to established ones, our brave churches can care for people who live with infertility or have experienced miscarriage. Our churches can be sensitive to the choices that couples make—to live child-free or to become parents in any number of ways. Though Hannah's story in scripture ended with a baby, not every person who wants a baby will have one.

Infertility can disappoint dreams of parenthood. Miscarriages don't always lead to rainbow babies. Couples who reach the dead end of fertility treatments don't always "just adopt." Not every story has a happy ending. No matter where the story ends, brave churches can offer compassion for the journey.

BRAVE TALK

1. Reread the story of Hannah in 1 Samuel 1:1-20. Have you or someone you know ever longed for a child? How does Hannah's story mirror that experience? In what ways does it differ? How does infertility or miscarriage shape these stories and their outcome?
2. What do you think stops people from talking about infertility or miscarriage? What settings might encourage more people to share these stories?
3. What weekly or yearly church activities might cause pain for a person who is living with infertility or who has recently experienced a miscarriage?
4. Consider the way your church celebrates Mother's Day and Father's Day. How do these celebrations encourage or discourage members of your church? How might you observe these holidays with greater intentionality and compassion for all church members?
5. How might your congregation provide support and care for couples grieving for children they have lost or children they don't yet have?

BRAVE ACT

Did you know that the second Sunday of November is known as Orphan Sunday?[16] Consider marking the occasion on your church calendar. Invite a speaker from a local adoption or foster care agency. Share statistics about children who are displaced from their family of birth. Raise money to support an organization providing care to children living in foster care.

CHAPTER 3

Let's Talk About Mental Illness

I am overwhelmed with troubles and my life draws near to death.
I am counted among those who go down to the pit; I am like one without strength.
I am set apart with the dead, like the slain who lie in the grave,
whom you remember no more, who are cut off from your care.
You have put me in the lowest pit, in the darkest depths.
Your wrath lies heavily on me; you have overwhelmed me with all your waves.
You have taken from me my closest friends and have made me repulsive to them.

—PSALM 88:3-8, NIV

*S*everal years ago, I worshiped with a community of monks at an abbey. Psalm 88 was included in the evening prayer. As the monks chanted the psalmist's words, I felt the temptation to look at my watch, wondering how long it would go on. The monks chanted these painful words *so slowly*. But as I continued to listen, I came to realize how powerful it was to hear the psalm read by a community. Though we might be tempted to interpret Psalm 88 as an individual experience of sorrow (which may or may not be ours right now), the monks' recitation invited all of us to share in this experience. In the community of God, your sorrow is my sorrow. And my sorrow is yours. Our pain is shared.

To live with a mental illness is to feel worried, confused, overwhelmed, lost, and alone. Experiencing mental illness, you might sense that your mind is working against your best interests or that your thoughts about the world cannot be trusted. Like any other medical condition, mental illness is not a choice and cannot be avoided when it arrives. For some people, the experience of mental illness is temporary; it may be triggered by a life change or passing challenge. For others, mental illness requires the ongoing attention of health-care professionals. It can be a chronic condition and, in some cases, one that might lead people to take their own lives. Mental illness must be taken seriously.

Giving voice to the experience of depression, anxiety, fear, and listlessness, Psalm 88 could be titled "The Saddest Song in the Bible." We don't know much about the author, but we recognize his ability to capture the anguish and isolation that can accompany mental illness. His mind overflows with thoughts of death. Feeling fragile and defenseless, he questions his purpose on earth and wonders what might happen if the waves of life continue to crash upon him. We can almost taste the psalmist's tears. We can feel his despair. We can see him withdrawing from a world that can't seem to handle his true emotions. He cries out, "Where is the hope? Does my life matter?"

We cry out together as we explore the topic of mental illness this session. When you gather your group, start with a few minutes of silence. Make space for the stories you will hear and hold in this time together. Consider how you might shoulder one another's burdens as you share in this communal experience of pain. Then, ask one group member to offer this prayer:

> *God, we cry out to you with open hearts. We ask for the courage to share our pain—to tell stories that may be difficult to tell, to hear stories we might not want to hear, and to listen for the gifts our struggles can bring. We want to be a community that can sing sad songs. We want to be a community that does real life together. Amen.*

BRAVE EXPLORATION

Let's start with the basics. What is mental illness? The Centers for Disease Control and Prevention (CDC) answers: "Mental illnesses are conditions that affect a person's thinking, feeling, mood, or behavior."[1] These conditions can range in severity; most have mild effects, but some can cause serious impairments. A serious mental illness, or condition that "substantially interferes with or limits one or more major life activities," usually requires assistance from health-care professionals, medication, and prescribed patterns of living.[2] Types of mental illness include depression and other mood disorders, anxiety disorders, attention-deficit/hyperactivity disorder (ADHD), post-traumatic stress disorder, personality disorders, schizophrenia spectrum disorders, and substance use disorders. To talk about mental illness is to talk about a wide array of experiences—more than the typical ups and downs that come with being human.

Mental illness is a common health condition in the United States. One in five Americans experiences mental illness each year.[3] One in twenty-five Americans lives with a serious mental illness. More than 50 percent of Americans will be diagnosed with a mental illness during their lifetime.[4] More than likely, you or someone you know has experienced mental illness. While some people experience temporary mental illness, others live with chronic (long-lasting) illnesses. Half of these chronic illnesses are diagnosed by the age of fourteen and three-quarters by the age of twenty-four. About one in five children has had a debilitating mental illness.[5] Mental illness does not discriminate; it affects senior citizens, middle-aged folks, young adults, teens, and children.

Yet, we rarely talk about mental illness in church. The taboo nature of the topic is illuminated by two recent studies. The first study, conducted by Amy Simpson in conjunction with *Leadership Journal* in 2010, surveyed 500 pastors and other church leaders. The study found that while 98.4 percent of church leaders are "aware of mental illnesses or disorders among people in their congregations," only 12.5 percent discuss mental illness "openly and in a healthy way in their churches."[6] The second study, conducted by LifeWay Research in partnership with Focus on the Family in 2014, surveyed 1,000 Protestant pastors. It found that 49 percent rarely or never speak about mental illness in sermons or large group messages.[7] The LifeWay study also surveyed 300 Protestants diagnosed with mental illnesses; only 53 percent said they felt supported by their churches, and 39 percent said their churches helped them to live out their faith in the context of their mental illness.[8]

More than likely, you have witnessed the church's silence on mental illness firsthand. If your church is anything like mine, you hear lots of requests during Sunday services to pray for "Aunt Judy who's having surgery next week" or for "My neighbor who just found out she has cancer." But you rarely hear prayer requests for someone who is clinically depressed or hospitalized for mental illness or struggling to pay for out-of-pocket therapists. We do not talk about the father with a newly diagnosed panic disorder or about the teen who tried to take his own life. Few people share these stories because we have not established the necessary bonds of trust within our congregations. Our churches don't feel safe, or perhaps aren't safe, for these concerns. We have work to do. As your group dives into this week's topic, consider how your church might carry more stories (and new stories) about people living with mental illness. The next few pages offer some questions for you to ponder and ideas for you to explore.

How Can We Remove the Stigma Around Mental Illness?

Words have the power to harm or to heal. How we talk about mental illness—the language we use—can shape the conversations we have. Consider the slang we use to describe people who may (or may not) be experiencing mental illness. For example, you might have heard someone's behavior described as *psycho* or *loony*. If you live in the South, where I'm from, you may have heard the colloquial phrase, *They're just not right*. This kind of language creates a sense of otherness and reinforces the stigma around mental illness. Who would feel comfortable talking about their experience of mental illness if they knew that they would be labeled in such a way? Fearing the stigma, many people remain silent.

Fear, of course, is what creates the stigma around mental illness in the first place. We use otherness language to talk about what we fear or don't understand—in this case, mental illness. Yet, when we use these words to talk about *people*, we make it harder to gain the insight that might ease our fears; this language makes it harder for us to see the person beyond the illness. A person living with bipolar disorder told me once that he wished folks wouldn't call him *crazy* or *irrational*. He went on to say, "I just need medication. For anyone who takes medication, it works when you use it. It doesn't if you don't. That is all." Labels create false distinctions between us. By using otherness language to talk about mental illness, we stop conversations—and the potential for meaningful relationships—before they begin.

To begin removing the fear and stigma, we can educate ourselves about mental illness. We might start by researching common myths and stereotypes. For instance, many people believe that mental illness causes violent behavior. This stereotype couldn't be further from the truth. Most people with mental illness are not violent; in fact, people who live with mental illness are far more likely to be the victims than the perpetrators of violent crimes.[9] Busting these myths can help to inform us about the facts of mental illness and allow us to see people beyond their diagnoses. If someone you know has a mental illness, you could do research to understand what they might be experiencing. But the best source of information might be that person. You could ask, "Would you be willing to tell me more about depression?" Being honest about the limits of your knowledge and asking respectful questions can set the stage for an open and loving conversation.

Before you start talking about mental illness with your group, you may want to discuss what respectful language sounds like in this conversation. Beyond avoiding derogatory slang and labels, it may be useful to adopt person-first language that places the person before the condition or illness. For instance, instead of saying "the mentally ill" or "sufferers," you might say, "people who are living with mental illness."[10] Ask your group members if they have any language preferences. Use the language that is right for your group and that ensures all your group members feel valued. Recognize that you may slip and say the wrong thing; don't let that stop the conversation. Talking together as people with different experiences is the most critical step to breaking down the stigma around mental illness.

How Do We Start Talking About Mental Illness?

Silence breeds silence. If no one is talking openly about their experiences with mental health, no one wants to be the first person to test the waters and see how the community responds. I understand this fear. I too have been scared to share my experience with mental illness. As a pastor, I feared telling members of my congregation that I had been diagnosed with situational depression during my years of infertility. I didn't know if they would trust me with their concerns if they knew I was taking medication for a chemical imbalance. I have feared also for a few of my family members who have been diagnosed with serious mental illnesses; I have worried that they might be ostracized from their faith communities if they revealed the extent of their disorders. I am a church leader. If I have been scared of speaking up about my personal experiences with mental illness, I only can imagine the fear other members of the congregation must feel.

When we share our stories with other people, we do so without knowing how they will respond. Will they empathize and accept us for who we are? Will they condemn us and walk away? Sharing of ourselves—particularly our challenges with mental illness—leaves us vulnerable. Social researcher Brené Brown defines *vulnerability* as "uncertainty, risk, and emotional exposure."[11] While that exposure can be uncomfortable and even scary, Brown insists that vulnerability is vital for human connection: "Vulnerability is the birthplace of love, belonging, joy, courage, and creativity. It is the source of hope, empathy, accountability, and authenticity. If we want greater clarity in our purpose or deeper or more meaningful spiritual lives, vulnerability is the path."[12] When we censor our stories, we may secure a temporary emotional safety, but we miss the opportunity to partake in the expansive love and support our community can provide. Becoming a brave church means accepting the uncertainty of vulnerability; it means taking a risk and speaking up about our personal experiences.

We need more church leaders willing to take the risk, to embrace vulnerability. We need pastors, deacons, and elders who are willing to be the first to share their mental health challenges. We need small group facilitators and Sunday school teachers willing to lead with the courage of an open heart. As silence breeds silence, so vulnerability invites vulnerability. When one church member tests the safety of the sanctuary by offering an earnest prayer request for a friend who has been hospitalized for mental illness, it encourages another person to offer a similar concern the next Sunday. When a minister calls attention to the presence of mental illness, it invites worshippers to share their own experiences. With this kind of courageous leadership, we inspire new conversations and connections in our congregations.

What Is the Role of Prayer in Responding to Mental Illness?

As we make room for new voices to be heard, we also can find new ways to respond to stories of mental illness. In particular, we can reexamine the role of prayer. As Christians, we know that God calls us to pray for those who are hurting (see Philippians 2:4). But for people suffering from mental illness, miraculous healing is not always possible. As Ed Stetzer, the Billy Graham Distinguished Chair of Church, Mission, and Evangelism at Wheaton College, writes, "We have all seen people, even believers, struggle with severe mental problems. They affect them emotionally, spiritually, and relationally, and sometimes deliverance does not seem to come in supernatural ways."[13] Despite earnest prayer, devout Christians can grapple with serious mental illness for their entire lives.

We can do great harm when we insist that prayer is the only answer to mental illness. A former parishioner at my church lives with an eating disorder. He shared with me his tally sheet—how many times well-meaning Christians have offered to pray for him when he speaks about his struggles. One fellow churchgoer even suggested that he wouldn't need therapy if he trusted God more. All the talk of prayer and trust, he said, can make him feel less than the spiritually grounded person he considers himself to be. He believes his life is saved over and over again by the ongoing gift of psychotherapy. In other words, prayer is a ritual that helps us know God is present with us. Prayer in action may look like therapy.

Even with prayer, therapy, medication, and health care, faithful Christians do not always find healing. In 2013, Rick Warren, the pastor of an evangelical church in Lake Forest, California, announced that his son, Matthew, died by suicide at age twenty-seven. In a letter to his congregation at Saddleback Church, Warren wrote about his son: "He struggled from birth with mental illness, dark holes of depression, and even suicidal thoughts. In spite of America's best doctors, meds, counselors, and prayers for healing, the torture of mental illness never subsided."[14] Matthew Warren—with access to medical care and what some might consider the best spiritual guidance—did not find relief from mental illness in his lifetime.

Matthew's death became an invitation for the church. In an editorial published in *Time* magazine in 2014, Rick and Kay Warren wrote, "Mental illness took our son's life, as it did many of the 38,000 other Americans who took their lives last year, but we refuse to let his death be just another statistic."[15] To honor his life, they hosted an event that explored the church's role in caring for and ministering to people living with mental illness. The Gathering on Mental Health and Care took place at Saddleback and resulted in the church's ongoing mental health ministry. The Warrens urged other churches to join them in offering compassion, acceptance, and love to people living with mental illness.

How Do We Extend God's Love to Those with Mental Illness?

We are all welcome at the table of God—even with mental illness. Churches are created for community, and community—that deep sense of belonging—is so important when we are experiencing the isolation of mental illness. Jesus came to help those who were sick (see Luke 4:40). As followers of Christ, we are called to extend God's unconditional love to all people, especially to those who are suffering from any kind of illness. Yet, our churches so often fail to support or even recognize people who are experiencing mental illness. As we identify our shortfalls and missed opportunities, we can find new ways to expand and deepen our ministries.

Few churches have ministries or support services devoted to mental health. When I began writing this book, I asked denominational leaders to point me toward churches with vital mental illness ministries. In response, I received lists of churches with robust *homeless* ministries. Certainly, feeding and sheltering people experiencing homelessness is a wonderful, Christ-centered activity (see Matthew 25:35-36). And connections do exist between homelessness and mental illness: People with untreated serious mental illnesses make up at least one-fourth of the homeless population, and a poorly managed mental illness may increase a person's risk of becoming homeless.[16] But to conflate homelessness and mental illness is to perpetuate stereotypes. No, mental illness is not just "a homeless thing."

Many of the well-dressed homeowners in our pews are living with mental illness. Mental illness has nothing to do with how faithful we are, how loved we are, how educated we are, or how much money we make. Yet, perhaps in an effort to appear as "blessed and highly favored" Christians, we like to pretend that mental illness does not exist inside our sanctuaries. In *Troubled Minds: Mental Illness and the Church's Mission*, Amy Simpson recalls how her church responded when her mother was diagnosed with schizophrenia: "I had the sense that people knew what was going on and didn't want to acknowledge it—which may or may not be true. I also got the message that more information would not be welcome, and I should be ashamed and keep my mouth shut."[17] Since no one seemed willing to talk about it, Simpson stopped trying. People often don't know what to say or how to help someone affected by mental illness. But by refusing to acknowledge the experience at all, we deepen the isolation of people who may already feel different and alone.

We can do better. We can do more. Consider how, at a moment's notice, church care teams can coordinate homecooked meals for parishioners recovering from surgery, organize visits to homebound church members, or collect money to help pay for hospital bills. How does your church respond when a parishioner is admitted to a psychiatric hospital? What happens when a church member returns home from a rehab center? How do you help people struggling to pay for psychotherapy? Our most basic church rituals can include people experiencing mental illness. Just a little encouragement can go a long way, Simpson notes in *Troubled Minds*. While most of the members of the congregation (pastors included) kept their distance from her family, Simpson said her parents took comfort in the relationships they developed with a few church members—the people who drove her mom to appointments or who made time to listen as her dad processed his thoughts. These relationships made her parents feel less alone.[18] Having people who are not afraid of mental illness, who are comfortable talking about it, can make all the difference.

BRAVE CHURCH

Brave churches acknowledge the presence of mental illness and encourage parishioners to speak openly about their struggles. The two churches described in the next pages have found ways to support people who are affected by mental illness. Recognizing that mental illnesses manifest in many different ways, these churches know that one-size-fits-all solutions will not work. Instead, they respond creatively and flexibly to the specific needs of their communities.

New City Church in Minneapolis, Minnesota

A recent United Methodist Church plant, New City Church prioritizes the mental health of its congregation. The church knows that long Minnesota winters can trigger the onset of seasonal affective disorder, a type of depression that commonly affects people who live farther north where daylight hours are shorter. Recognizing the presence of the winter blues and clinical depression, church leaders organize parties and other social events that allow parishioners to connect during the cold, dark months. In addition, Rev. Tyler Sit makes it his pastoral policy to encourage therapy. "Church is not therapy, and therapy is not church," Sit believes. "We need both."[19] Encouraging therapy means making resources accessible. The church website offers a list of local mental health providers as well as information about their insurance policies.[20] It also provides information about the church's new mental health initiative, the Incarnation Fund.

Started in 2019, New City Church's Incarnation Fund aims to make therapy available to persons of color. The church community includes many people who experience discrimination because of their race, gender, or sexual orientation. Through the Incarnation Fund, the church hopes to provide its parishioners with support services from queer-affirming practitioners of color in the Minneapolis community. When I interviewed Sit in 2019, he said the Incarnation Fund would offer spiritual direction, nature-based therapy, and somatic experiencing (trauma therapy). He also said that because the program is still in an early stage of its development, it may change as the church grows and adapts to meet the needs of its community.[21] This brave church is not afraid to talk about mental illness. Before parishioners even have to ask, New City provides support and makes local resources available.

Christ Episcopal Church in Charlotte, North Carolina

Another church that has broken the silence on mental health is Christ Episcopal Church in Charlotte, North Carolina. Founded in 1943, Christ Episcopal serves a congregation of over six thousand members and strives to meet the unique needs of this large community.[22] The church began its mental health ministry in 2008 with a Sunday morning forum called "The Wisdom of Contentment." Recognizing the painful effects the financial crisis and recession might have on its affluent congregation, the church offered this forum as a way for parishioners to talk about their struggles. Leaders were stunned by the congregation's response; one after the other, members spoke up about not only financial problems but also emotional and spiritual concerns. "It made our pain so public and so widely shared," said Rev. Chip Edens. "It opened us up more deeply to the struggles of our members."[23] Everyone struggles, Christ Episcopal learned together; the congregation now believes no one should struggle alone.

The bonds of trust they built during the forum proved essential when the congregation mourned six suicides in five years. As they grieved their losses, the congregation took action. The church began hosting Survivors of Suicide (SOS), a support group open to the community. "The act of sharing stories with others, sharing grief with others, is therapeutic," said Jon Kocmond, a parishioner whose teenage son Nathan died by suicide in 2017. "If we need love to overcome sorrow, what greater source than God?"[24] In addition to providing grief support, Christ Episcopal organized an annual speaker series on topics of mental illness. In 2019, the congregation welcomed a new wellness director, who provides short-term counseling services and connects people experiencing mental health challenges with local service providers and other resources.[25] This brave church continues to invest in mental health support for its community, and the programs they provide help people to know they are loved and accepted.

Christ Episcopal Church and New City Church have been working to remove the stigma around mental illness. The pastors of these churches lead with vulnerability. By starting the conversation about mental illness and offering support services, they have created an environment that allows parishioners to talk about their own struggles and to ask for the help they need. These brave churches extend God's love, acceptance, and compassion to people affected by mental illness.

BRAVE TALK

1. One in five Americans will experience mental illness this year. What keeps you from talking about mental illness? Are you (or your congregation) afraid of the topic?
2. What are some slang expressions used to describe mental illness? (A few examples: "He's so crazy." "She went to the loony bin." "I saw my shrink today.") How does this language affect your conversations? As your group begins to talk about mental illness, what language will you agree to use? What language will you avoid?
3. What is the role of prayer in the context of mental illness? How can your church put prayer into action for parishioners who live with mental illness?
4. What is one church tradition or ritual that your congregation could rewrite or reformulate to be more sensitive to people experiencing mental illness? What new traditions could you create?
5. Discuss the mental health ministries at New City Church and Christ Episcopal Church. What ideas can you take from these examples? How can you support people with mental illness in your church and community? What are the most pressing needs?

BRAVE ACT

Identify a few church members who can complete training in Mental Health First Aid and can share the information they learn with your congregation. Countless mental health professionals recommended this course to me as an essential first step to starting a mental health ministry. It provides the information you need to identity, understand, and respond to signs of mental illness. You can find more at https://www.mentalhealthfirstaid.org/.

CHAPTER 4

Let's Talk About Domestic Violence

My heart is in anguish within me, the terrors of death
have fallen upon me.
Fear and trembling come upon me, and horror over-
whelms me.
And I say, "O that I had wings like a dove! I would fly
away and be at rest."
It is not enemies who taunt me—I could bear that;
it is not adversaries who deal insolently with me—I could
hide from them.
But it is you, my equal, my companion, my familiar friend,
with whom I kept pleasant company.

—PSALM 55:4-6, 12-14

Sweat pools on your brow. Your pulse quickens. Your heart races, and adrenaline courses through your veins. You must get out right now. But you can't. Your partner's car just pulled into the garage. You're trapped. Anyone who has experienced domestic violence knows all too

well the surge of fear that occurs at home—a place that should be safe.
Isn't that true? We design our homes to be places of retreat. We go
home to escape from the world, to relax and let down our guard. We
trust our houses to shelter us from the elements of the natural world.
We build fences around them to keep out unwanted guests. But what if
our homes cannot protect us? What if the danger cannot be kept out by
locks, gates, or security systems? What if the threat comes from within?
What do we do then? How do we live when our homes aren't safe?

David describes this fear in Psalm 55. While we do not know the
particularities of his situation, we can gather from his writing that David
is afraid of someone he used to trust.[1] The fear consumes his mind, and
his heart starts to race. When the violence ensues, David endures by dis-
sociating; in his mind, he flies to a safe place with "wings like a dove."
He is shocked. We can hear the pain of betrayal: "It is you, my equal,
my companion, my familiar friend" (Ps. 55:13). David didn't expect
a threat to emerge from the community of support that he'd chosen.
People who experience domestic violence today feel this same terror,
shock, and betrayal. They wonder, *How did this happen to me?*

As you gather with your group, take a moment to consider your
own family and friends. Do you know someone who has experienced
domestic violence? Maybe that someone is you. Pause in silence to
honor this person's experience and to pray for healing from the trauma
of abuse. Then, ask one group member to offer this invocation:

> *God, we never know what goes on behind closed doors. Soften our
> hearts as we consider the terror of this violence that is so often
> endured in secrecy. Deepen our empathy as we hear stories that may
> seem unfathomable to us. Embolden us to speak up for those who
> are afraid to speak up for themselves. Amen.*

BRAVE EXPLORATION

I will never forget the call I got one afternoon from my friend Amber.[2]
Though we now lived hundreds of miles apart, Amber and I had grown

up together. I knew her parents, and she knew mine. I officiated her wedding and baptized her first baby, Jonathan. I held a lot of respect for the ways she and her husband, Jared, spent their time volunteering in their community and supporting environmental protection programs. I visited their home many times, and I always was impressed with how orderly it was. Colorful airplane stencils brightened their son's bedroom. Happy photographs from family vacations lined their hallways. Amber was the last person I imagined would call me in a panic to say, "I left my husband. Jonathan and I are in a shelter. The abuse was more than I could take anymore. I saw him hit Jonathan too."

Domestic violence, or intimate partner violence, is a leading public health threat in the United States. The CDC defines intimate partner violence as "violence or aggression that occurs in a close relationship."[3] It can include any act of physical violence, sexual violence, stalking, or psychological aggression that occurs between current or former spouses or within dating relationships.[4] This chapter focuses on the abuse that occurs in marriages and particularly on the violence against women. However, partner abuse extends beyond the home and effects people of all ages, economic statuses, races, sexual orientations, and gender identities.

Research shows that a staggering number of Americans have experienced some form of intimate partner violence in their lifetime. According to a CDC survey, one in five women and one in seven men report having experienced severe physical violence. About one in five women and one in twelve men have experienced sexual violence. More than 43 million women and 38 million men have experienced psychological aggression.[5] To make these numbers personal: Someone you know is experiencing or has experienced domestic violence. It may be the last person you would imagine it to be, and this person probably doesn't see help within reach.

We often picture abuse as bruised eyes and bloodied lips. However, domestic violence is any pattern of behavior used to maintain power and control in an intimate relationship; these behaviors include acts of not only physical violence but also emotional abuse and psychological aggression.[6] Rachel G. Hackenberg describes her experience of domestic violence this way: "I married a mean and abusive man. He criticized the way I walked. He was alternately annoyed and irate at the way I parented. He demanded the children's playful attention when he was in a good mood and their absolute silence when he was in a foul mood. He required my willingness to cook a full meal at any hour."[7] Hackenberg remained silent for many years about the emotional abuse she endured at home. She felt incapable of putting it into words at the time, and she still struggles to name many of her then-husband's specific behaviors.

Intimate partner violence is sometimes called a "silent epidemic." People struggle to talk about their experiences with abuse for many reasons—fear, embarrassment, and shame are only a few. I asked Amber, someone I know to be an intelligent and articulate woman, why she delayed asking for help. "I didn't think anyone would believe me," she replied. "To the world, we were the perfect couple." Like Amber, many people don't seek the support of friends because they don't think they will be taken seriously. Even fewer people call in law enforcement. Only 20 percent of all rapes and 25 percent of all assaults perpetrated against women are reported to the police. Most victims do not see the justice system as the place to address the abuse.[8]

As sites for community gathering, churches could be safe places to seek help. Pastors enthusiastically agree. A 2017 LifeWay Research poll that surveyed 1,000 Protestant pastors found that almost all pastors (98 percent) believed their church would be safe haven for people experiencing abuse.[9] Yet only half (52 percent) of the churches had a specific plan in place to help victims of abuse, and a little more than one-third (37 percent) of pastors knew of a person in their church who experienced domestic violence in the past three years.[10] The survey also found that if a church member cited domestic violence as the reason for divorce, only 56 percent of pastors would believe the claim and 60 percent would investigate it.[11] While our congregations may believe intimate partner violence is wrong and we may say we want to help people in crisis, these figures show us that our churches aren't always helping.

Sadly, in some cases, our churches may be doing harm. Conservative Christian blogger Natalie Hoffman is a mother of nine who survived decades of abuse. Now a life coach, Hoffman listens to the stories of Christian women who are trying to end abusive marriages. "I would venture a guess that only about 3–5 percent of them have support from their churches."[12] She goes on to suggest that the way many churches respond to women reporting domestic violence can be incredibly damaging—a form of spiritual abuse. Hoffman's blog highlights some responses she and other victims have heard: "You made a vow before God—for better or for worse. Your relationship will improve if you show more respect to your husband." With these kinds of responses, Hoffman argues, church leaders effectively blame the victim and allow the violence and abuse to continue.[13] Her assessment shows us we've got work to do.

As we develop plans to better care for victims and survivors of domestic violence, we can turn to experts for guidance. We can educate ourselves about intimate partner violence and ask our pastors to address the subject from the pulpit and in other church communications. We can identify safe places, service providers, and other relevant resources in our local communities. However, real change requires introspection. If our congregations want to support people who are experiencing domestic violence, I believe we need to take some time to explore our theological convictions and how they shape the way we respond to victims and survivors of abuse. To spark discussion and reflection, I offer three questions over the next few pages.

What Does Your Church Believe About Submission?

Many conservative churches believe that men should hold authority in the church and at home and that women should submit to their leadership. Submission theology, as it relates to marriage, draws on Ephesians 5:22-23. The statement of faith for the Southern Baptist Convention, *The Baptist Faith and Message,* echoes this verse in its amendment on family roles. Added in 1998, the amendment states, "A wife is to submit herself graciously to the servant leadership of her husband even as the church willingly submits to the headship of Christ."[14] Submission theology can lead, depending on its application, to the silencing of women who are abused by their husbands. Women may not speak up or seek help because they believe it's their Christian duty to submit to their abusive partners. Many victims blame themselves for the abuse; it wouldn't have happened if they were more submissive. Others choose to accept the violence as part of their marriage and the abuse as their cross to bear.

Some pastors do little to counter these insidious beliefs. Paige Patterson, the president of Southwestern Baptist Theological Seminary from 2003 to 2018, is known for his leadership in the 1998 revision of *The Baptist Faith and Message*. In an interview recorded in 2000 that resurfaced online in 2018, Patterson was asked what he tells women who are experiencing physical abuse from their husbands. He responded, "It depends on the level of abuse."[15] Patterson explained that only in the most serious cases he might recommend a temporary separation; he tells most women to pray. "Remember, when nobody else can help, God can," Patterson said. "And in the meantime, you have to do what you can at home to be submissive in every way that you can and to elevate [your husband]."[16] Patterson's statements sparked national criticism when the audio clip began circulating online. Though some Southern Baptist leaders defended Patterson, who said his words were being misconstrued, the Seminary asked him to step down from his position shortly after the controversy began.[17]

Many Christian leaders, however, have denounced the idea that women should endure violence and abuse in order to remain submissive to their partner. Rev. Dr. Leslie Copeland-Tune wrote her dissertation on clergywomen's experiences with domestic violence. In an article she published in 2015, she argues that submission should not be used to rationalize abuse: "God does not expect nor does God want us to submit to sin . . . God is not abusive. God is loving, kind, longsuffering, and full of mercy."[18] After the clip of Patterson sparked controversy, popular Christian author Beth Moore responded on Twitter: "I'm pro marriage. Nearly 40 years of ups and downs to back that up. But when we as a church culture demonize divorce as the worst possible outcome—the sin of all sins—we truly have no clue on this ever loving earth what some people are enduring. We do not submit to abuse. NO."[19] She's right. No one deserves to be abused. Our churches can find ways to uphold our beliefs about submission (whatever those may be) and to shelter women experiencing violence and abuse.

What Does Your Church Believe About Marriage and Divorce?

Marriage is a sacred covenant. Many Christians see divorce as a last resort; some do not consider it to be an option at all. Despite sometimes life-threatening violence, Christians who experience abuse often struggle to end their marriages. Many victims love their partners; they want the abuse to stop but the relationship to continue. And, as abusers often limit social contacts of their partners, victims cherish the friendships they can maintain. For many Christians, God is the only person they can talk to. When she considered ending her abusive marriage, Amber remembers receiving two verses from her pastor: "For I hate divorce, says the LORD" (Mal. 2:16); "So they are no longer two, but one flesh. Therefore what God has joined together, let no one separate" (Matt. 19:6). Like many Christians who wrestle with these verses, Amber heard them as a warning. She didn't want God to hate her too.

Some church leaders amplify that warning and threaten to withdraw church support. After years of abuse, Christian author and radio personality Autumn Miles filed for divorce. In an article published in *The Christian Century*, she described the way her church responded:

> At the age of twenty-two, after I finally mustered up the courage to file for divorce from the man who had injured me verbally and physically, the elders of our congregation sat us both down in the same room to confront what they felt like was my sin in choosing divorce. These men were individuals whom I had looked up to for my entire life, whose children I had babysat, who served alongside my father—the lead pastor of the church—who had been denied a seat at this meeting. With my then-husband in the room, my attempts to explain the desperation of my situation fell on hardened hearts. "If you go

through with this divorce," one of the elders told me, "God will never use you."[20]

When she and her husband divorced, the church forced Miles to retract her membership, and her father was dismissed from his position.[21] The stakes can be high for Christians looking for a way out of abusive relationships.

When Amber asked for help, her church answered with a warning. When Miles shared her story, her church gave her an ultimatum. When our churches hear stories of abuse and respond in these ways, victims of abuse receive this message: *Your marriage is more important to God than your life or the lives of your children. Even if you suffer or die at the hand of your partner, marriage vows should not be broken.* Brenda Branson and Paula J. Silva chastise churches for this kind of thinking. In *Violence Among Us: Ministry to Families in Crisis,* they write, "The safety of women and children should never be sacrificed on the altar of the institution of marriage."[22] While we own the impact of these destructive messages, Christians don't intend to harm victims of abuse. Our churches can lift up the virtues of marriage and communicate beliefs about divorce in a way that supports victims and survivors.

What Does Your Church Believe About Forgiveness and Reconciliation?

Forgiveness is essential to the Christian faith. From the Bible, we receive the central narrative of our faith: Despite our human failings, God forgives us. The Gospels tell us the story of Jesus' life, death, resurrection, and reconciliation with God. Scripture is full of stories about forgiveness. One of our most popular parables is the story of the prodigal son: A son messes up big time, but he realizes his mistakes; he comes home and asks for forgiveness from his father, who not only forgives him but also celebrates his return with a lavish party. This story offers a beautiful metaphor for God's grace. In our preaching and teaching, we often elevate the text as a model for Christian behavior.

Yet, consider how the parable of the prodigal son might speak to Christians who are experiencing intimate partner abuse; think about how it relates to stories they may have been telling themselves. The "cycle of abuse," as some psychologists call it, describes a pattern in abusive relationships: tensions build; an abusive incident occurs; the abuser apologizes, the abused forgives, and the couple reenters a honeymoon phase of their loving relationship—until the cycle starts again.[23] When a victim of abuse hears the story of the prodigal son lifted up as model behavior, they might hear that God wants them to forgive and reconcile, to enter again into a loving relationship with their abuser. When we teach this parable without consideration for victims who may be struggling to set physical and emotional boundaries, victims may believe that the church wants them to dissolve those boundaries and to stay in their abusive relationships, no matter what.

Sometimes pastors do encourage people experiencing abuse to stay in their marriages. When confronted by a parishioner who is describing acts of intimate partner violence, pastors often default into the mode of a couples' counselor with the aim of restoring the relationship. They often want to orchestrate reconciliation. They may listen closely to the victim's experiences and then ask him or her to consider forgiving the abusing partner. Then the pastor may talk with the abuser. The problem with this approach, according to Julie Owens, a consultant who designs domestic violence prevention programs, is that abusers know how to manipulate. They will tell pastors what they want to hear; they will deny the claim or repent and express an interest in repairing the relationship. Then, the abuser will retaliate at home; behind closed doors, the violence will escalate.[24] Even with the intent of pursuing and teaching Christian forgiveness and reconciliation, pastors can put victims of violence in even more dangerous situations.

Abusive marriages are difficult, if not impossible, to repair. It's important to understand that reconciliation simply isn't safe for many victims of domestic violence. "Churches underestimate the spiritual, psychological, and emotional damage done by domestic abuse," Owens said.[25] Couples counseling is not a useful option for most abusive relationships. It does not solve issues of power and control. In most cases, the relationships need to end, and survivors need time to heal.[26] To some survivors, forgiveness may feel like an insurmountable task or an unfair burden; they have done nothing wrong. The wounds of trauma and abuse cut deep. Forgiveness can take a long time; it may not happen at all. As we learn to support victims and survivors of domestic violence, our churches can accept that reconciliation may not be appropriate, and we can let survivors heal at their own pace. We can make a distinction between the grace of God and our own mortal means of love and forgiveness.

BRAVE CHURCH

Brave churches listen with intention to the stories that victims and survivors tell. Brave churches believe that the abuse took place and prioritize safety of the victim(s).[27] Instead of offering advice, they ask questions. They find out what the person experiencing that abuse needs. Brave churches admit their limitations; if pastors and parishioners are not equipped to provide the necessary care, they find organizations that can help.[28] Brave churches, like the two described over the next pages, offer support through thoughtful worship services, educational programs, and community outreach. These brave churches walk alongside victims and survivors of abuse.

Metro Baptist Church in New York, New York

Metro Baptist Church is committed to supporting survivors of domestic violence. When the congregation moved into a building in Hell's Kitchen in 1984, a church pamphlet proclaimed, "Homeless people down the block. Prostitutes on the corner. Crack dealers across the street. What a great place for a church."[29] The congregation went to work opening a food pantry, building a winter clothes closet, and then incorporating a nonprofit organization—Rauschenbusch Metro

Ministries. The nonprofit has continued to expand the church's social ministry, allowing Metro to serve its community seven days a week. Rauschenbusch's Living Well Life Skills Empowerment Program offers assistance to women who have experienced both domestic violence and homelessness. The Living Well program, originally developed by Catholic Charities, aims to reduce the effects of trauma and to improve coping skills. Participants meet for twenty-eight sessions in small groups of no more than ten women. During the fourteen-week program, the women receive education about trauma, talk about their experiences in guided conversations, and develop personal narratives to share at a closing ceremony.[30] Although the program does not include Bible study nor does it seek to change anyone's religious beliefs, members of Metro are deeply engaged with the program. They pray for the participants each Sunday, cook meals for the sessions, and serve as program mentors.

The church's involvement has been meaningful to many of the women who have participated in the program. Rev. Lesley-Ann Hix Tommey, a ministry facilitator for Living Well, described some of the responses she has received: "Participants have said they finally feel like they have a home, like they have a place to belong, like they've been forgiven. We had one woman who was very nervous to come to a church building for the group because she had been abused in a church community before. By the middle of the group, she pulled me aside and told me one night that she realized [that] we were different and good, that not all church people are bad. . . . She came back to her Christian faith by the end of our semester together. She is completely transformed and has so much joy."[31] Metro's Living Well program allows the church to be a space of healing for survivors of domestic violence and offers a way for the congregation to learn with and from these women.

Park Avenue Christian Church in New York City, New York

The Disciples of Christ congregation at Park Avenue Christian Church also creates space for conversations about intimate partner violence. The Park attracts a diverse group of parishioners with a median age of thirty-five. Executive Pastor Rev. Stephanie Kendell believes it's important not to make assumptions about what any group of people might need from the church. Rather than researching trends, she takes her cues from conversations that take place in church social programs. Rev. Kendell knew the church needed to break its silence on some seemingly taboo topics when she kept hearing young people repeat the phrase, "But what about . . .?"[32]

Intimate partner violence was the first topic of the new monthly Bible study in 2017. Led by Rev. Sydney Avent and Rev. Dr. Richard Sturm, the study examined biblical texts about violence against women. Recognizing the scripture readings and subsequent conversations might elicit trauma responses from victims and survivors, the pastors invited a licensed therapist to be present during the study. They didn't want to risk opening wounds without providing on-site professional care—a practice that has become standard during the church's continued ministry around intimate partner violence.[33] The Park puts the topic of domestic violence on the church calendar throughout the year.

The worship team at Park Avenue also makes a point of incorporating biblical texts and sermon illustrations that speak to the terror of violence and domestic abuse. Pastors are not afraid to name intimate partner violence as a sin and to bring into the pulpit the hard tales of abuse that are often overlooked in the lectionary.[34] "Speaking truth to power is pastoral care," Kendell said. "Speak the truth, even when it's hard or inconvenient. That is what your people need to hear."[35] When church leaders started talking about intimate partner violence, parishioners began talking about their own experiences with abuse. The conversations that have occurred after services and during Bible studies have helped to build the trust that makes pastoral care possible.

The Park and Metro Baptist both speak up about intimate partner violence and invite parishioners to share their own stories. These brave churches listen with intention and support victims and survivors of abuse.

BRAVE TALK

1. Briefly describe your connection to or knowledge of domestic violence in your own community. Refer again to the guidelines you set in the group covenant before sharing your own experiences or the experiences of others.
2. Why do you think you are shocked when you learn someone that you know is experiencing abuse? (You might think, *No, that couldn't have happened to this person or in this church or in this neighborhood!*) What can your disbelief tell you about the nature of domestic violence?
3. This chapter poses three theological questions that may affect how your church responds to people experiencing domestic abuse. Which concept(s) do you think you need more time to consider: submission, divorce, or forgiveness and reconciliation? Why?
4. If someone from your church told you that he or she was in an abusive relationship, how would you respond? If you need suggestions, you might dig into one of the resources listed in the back of the book.
5. How can your church provide more support to people experiencing intimate partner violence? After today's conversation, what's the first step you will take?

BRAVE ACT

Make plans to observe Domestic Violence Awareness Month in October. Put it on your church calendar now. Check out the resources listed in the back of this book that can help you to educate yourself and your congregation about intimate partner violence. Then, to increase your church's awareness, you might consider one or all of these ideas: Make purple ribbons for everyone in the congregation to wear. Insert flyers into the church bulletin about how and where to seek help in your community. Invite a trained counselor to speak to the emotional journey of people who experience domestic violence.

CHAPTER 5

Let's Talk About Racism

"Why do you see the speck in your neighbor's eye, but do not notice the log in your own eye? Or how can you say to your neighbor, 'Let me take the speck out of your eye,' while the log is in your own eye?"

—MATTHEW 7:3-4

hen you meet people, what do you notice first? What thoughts come next? You might notice the grocery store clerk speaks with a British accent or the bank teller has a Southern drawl. You may observe that your trainer at the gym has a lot of tattoos or that your hairstylist has multiple piercings. Or you might perceive your coworker as Black or your child's teacher as Hispanic. Before you know it, stories and associations flood your mind; these small observations often lead us to stereotypes and assumptions about what kind of people are before us. Without thinking consciously, our observations are filtered through stereotypes and our own latent biases. We make quick judgments and label the people we meet, both positively and negatively, without knowing their stories.

Jesus asks us to consider the way we perceive one another. In his Sermon on the Mount, he contrasts our quickness to judge our neighbor with our reluctance to observe our own biases. Jesus invites us to turn our attention to our blind spots—the "logs" that lead to misperceptions and unfair judgments. As you start to talk about racism with your group, commit to examining your blind spots and biases. Resist the impulse to label other people. Nothing will shut down this conversation faster than calling people "racist" or making assumptions about people based on their racial identity. While your discussion may lead you to challenge ideas, remember that you are not here to judge your group members. You are here to take a hard look at your own story. You are here to explore the ways your story has shaped your perceptions and to become aware of the "log" in your eye. You are here to see people anew.

You might begin this session with a time of silence to allow group members to reflect on the thoughts or feelings that arise when they hear the words *race* and *racism*, on how race has shaped their experiences, or on how racism has been a part of their lives. Share with one another any concerns or fears that arise at the prospect of talking about racism. Then, invite a group member to say this prayer:

> *God, your presence radiates throughout this room as we come together today. We come to make space in our hearts for new stories. Give us the courage to recognize our biases, and help us to let go of the prejudices that hinder our ability to see one another clearly. Expand our vision of what it means to become a beloved community. Amen.*

BRAVE EXPLORATION

I can remember the first time I thought about race. It was the mid-1980s, and I was a child living in a small town in Tennessee. Though I had learned in Sunday school that God loves all the people of the world,

I'd had little exposure to people of color. Most of my world was white. White parents. White neighbors. White church friends. Then, in my first-grade class at the public elementary school I attended, I met two girls with black skin, Mia and Tasha. I liked Tasha especially. We both loved laughing in the lunchroom and all things My Little Pony. But I noticed when I hung out with Mia and Tasha on the jungle gym during recess that the other kids in my class looked at me like I was weird. Or maybe I felt weird? For the first time, I became very aware of my white skin. When I asked my mom what it meant to have friends who were Black, she encouraged me to be friends with any kids I liked. However, you need to know this: I don't know when I stopped playing with Mia and Tasha, but it seemed easier to play with the kids who looked like me. This childhood memory makes me sad.

Our awareness of race can be startling when it first occurs (and when it keeps occurring over our lifetime). For the better part of my childhood, I did not have to think about race; I did not have to think about the color of my skin or the way people might perceive it. The color of my skin allowed me to blend in with everyone else in my rural Tennessee town; I could just be. I did not have to fear what names might be hurled at my family when we walked through town or ate at a local restaurant. I did not have to fear what the police might do if my parents were pulled over for speeding. I did not have to fear what assumptions people at school would make—that I would need free lunch or that I would be a troublemaker. I did not have these fears because my skin is white. From our first breath to our last, race and its societal implications shape our stories. I imagine some of you have stories similar to my own. I also imagine, however, that some of you have not had the privilege of ignoring race. I imagine some of you heard "the talk" from your parents and learned how your teachers, classmates, or friends' parents might treat you differently because your skin is brown or black. I imagine some of you have experienced prejudice and discrimination; maybe some of you, or a family member, have been the victim of racially motivated hate crime.

While we have had different experiences of race, as Christians, we know that racism has no place in the neighborhood Jesus asks us to create. Hate is not one of our faith languages—love is. Scripture tells us over and over again that we are people marked by love. We are loved unconditionally by God, and we are called to love others (see Matthew 10:37-38). Jesus confronted prejudice and discrimination, and he consistently welcomed the marginalized in his Jewish world. For example, women were viewed as second-class citizens in his day; yet, Jesus lifts up one particular woman as a hero in his teachings (see Luke 10:38-42). Samaritans were snubbed for their religious practices and sharply segregated from the Jews; yet, Jesus asks a Samaritan woman for a drink of water (see John 4:7-10). Lepers, people suffering from a skin disease, were seen as sinful and forced to live outside of town; yet, Jesus approaches the lepers, listens to their cries, touches and heals them (see Luke 17:11-19). As followers of Jesus, we are called to serve before we are served (see Mark 10:43-45) and to love as Christ first loved us (see John 13:34). This love is not charity for people we consider inferior in some way; as the apostle Paul reminds us, we are "equal with each other" (Gal. 3:28, CEV). We are all children of God.

Yet, faithful church-going folk often disagree about the scope of racism and the forms it takes in practice. A healthy conversation begins with agreed upon language and definitions. We are all learning how deeply rooted racism is in our personal beliefs and our institutions. Let us begin looking at a simple definition from *Merriam-Webster.* Then we will look at more nuanced concepts that help us see the ways racism lives in and among us at the individual and corporate level. *Racism,* as defined by *Merriam-Webster,* is "a belief that race is a fundamental determinant of human traits and capacities and that racial differences produce an inherent superiority of a particular race."[1] The dictionary also defines it as "behavior or attitudes that reflect and foster this belief: racial discrimination and prejudice."[2] Simply put, racism is belief and action. Using this basic dictionary definition, we likely can come to some consensus as we identity forms of overt racism. We can condemn individual acts of violent racism, like the mass shooting in 2015 when a white nationalist killed nine African Americans during a Bible study at Emanuel African Methodist Episcopal Church in Charleston, South Carolina. We can denounce hate groups, like the Ku Klux Klan, that rally behind explicitly racist beliefs about the superiority of the white race. We can lament corporate acts of racism in our nation's history, like the practices of slavery and segregation, practices supported by racist beliefs that were codified into law. But when we venture beyond these examples of blatant discrimination and hate, our collective understanding of racism becomes murkier.

Racism can be hard to pin down when our actions are not motivated by overt racist beliefs or when the impact of our actions does not align with our intentions. As Christians, we have a responsibility to consider the following concepts: implicit bias (individual actions can unconsciously and unintentionally reflect and foster racism); systemic racism (attitudes toward different racial groups affects the structure of our society); and historic racism (confronting racism today requires us to make amends for the past). In this brave space, I encourage you to consider how the impact of your actions might not always align with your intentions. The questions that follow offer your group a way to start exploring these ideas.

- **Implicit bias:** How might racism be present when we identify people by their race (i.e. "my Black friend")? How might racism be reflected in the decision to avoid driving through a reservation? How might racism be perpetuated by the choice to live in a homogenous neighborhood because "it's safer" or to send your children to a homogenous private school for a "better education"?
- **Systemic racism:** How might racism have led to disproportionate rates of homelessness among people of color? How might racial bias have contributed to your vocational achievements or lack thereof? How might racist attitudes affect the way you are treated in stores? How might racial bias have led police officers and criminal prosecutors to fill prisons with people of color?
- **Historic racism:** How might the trauma of slavery be inherited? How might you be participating in racism if your great-great-great grandfather owned a plantation? How might statues of Confederate soldiers promote or perpetuate racist ideals? How

might racism be condoned by the choice to live on land that was taken unjustly from people of another race? How might confronting racism require us to make amends for the past?

The past year has brought a renewed urgency to these conversations about racism, despite our disagreements on the topic. National demands for racial justice have followed in the wake of George Floyd's death. The forty-six-year-old Black man died after being arrested for a misdemeanor in Minneapolis, Minnesota, in May 2020. A white police officer knelt on his neck for eight minutes and forty-five seconds—despite Floyd begging, "Please, please, please" and saying over and over, "I can't breathe." He was not the first person of color to die in an encounter with the police. We can name many others: Philando Castile, Stephon Clark, Breonna Taylor, Eric Garner, and the list goes on. You may have different perspectives about what led to these individual deaths: Is the story about a few bad police officers or about deep-seated racism in our nation? But we have to ask ourselves why we keep seeing the same story of unarmed Black men and women being killed by police.

The harrowing images of Floyd's death cannot be unseen. His death, which some have called a "modern-day lynching,"[3] begs us to at least explore the ideas of implicit bias and systemic racism and to confront the sin of racism in its many insidious forms. Brave churches, we need to find ways to hear one another and to peel back the racism we can't yet see in our own hearts. We need to find ways to build the communities Jesus calls us to create, communities that welcome and respect people of all colors of skin, communities that proclaim those lives matter. As you start talking, I offer you two suggestions: acknowledge the single stories you've been told about race and commit to the discomfort of the conversation.

Acknowledge the Single Stories That You've Been Told About Race

The stories we've been told about race and stereotypes we hold have the power to harm. Novelist Chimamanda Ngozi Adichie gave a TED talk in 2009 called "The Danger of a Single Story."[4] In her talk, she describes learning to read in Enugu, Nigeria, and recalls that all of the children's books available to her came from American and British authors. She loved the books and how they transported her to a world beyond her own. However, as she read only these books, she received a single story about acceptable literature. When she began to write her own stories, her characters ate apples (something Adichie had never tasted) and played in the snow (something Adichie had never seen). By the time she moved to the United States for college, she knew a lot about Americans. But her college roommate knew only one story of Africans, and it often clashed with Adichie's lived experience. "[My roommate] asked if she could listen to what she called my 'tribal music' and was consequently very disappointed when I produced my tape of Mariah Carey."[5] Picturing Africans living in the bush, her roommate had a hard time hearing that Adichie grew up in a middle-class family with hired household help, that she knew how to use a stove, and that she came from a country called Nigeria, not Africa. Adichie reminds us that each story we've heard is simply *a* story and that a single story can be destructive when told alone.

Author and journalist Ta-Nehisi Coates also cautions against stereotypes. He asks his readers to set aside the single story they may have been told about Black boys in America—the story of rough and tough boys being raised in the projects by poor single mothers. In "Letter to My Son," Coates asks us to make room for another story: "Always remember that Trayvon Martin was a boy, that Tamir Rice was a particular boy, that Jordan Davis was a boy, like you. When you hear these names think of all the wealth poured into them. Think of the gasoline expended, the treads worn carting him to football games, basketball tournaments, and Little League. Think of the time spent regulating sleepovers. Think of the surprise birthday parties, the day care, and the reference checks on babysitters."[6] Coates reminds us that no single story about race can sum up an individual: You are not "Black people" or "white people." You are one person who is loved and valued. Our lives are full of complexities, contradictions, and sometimes conflicting stories— all of which are true. As you reflect on your personal experiences, I imagine you would agree. How would you feel if you met a new person and only got to tell one story to summarize your life? And what if the story that person heard wasn't even your story but one told about your race or ethnicity?

As we turn to our faith, we realize the Bible is also full complex and sometimes contradictory stories about the life of Jesus. Consider how each Gospel was written with a different audience in mind. For instance, Matthew wrote for a Jewish community and Luke for the non-Jewish Christians. As these writers tell the story of Jesus' life, the Gospels include different people, describe distinct scenes, and present unique perspectives. Each Gospel offers a new ending for the story of Jesus' resurrection. These seemingly conflicting stories—all of which are true—form the foundation of our faith. In the same way, when we start talking about race and racism, we can make room for stories that might conflict with our own experience, stories that give us a new perspective on the truth, stories that bring us together as followers of Christ in a diverse community of faith.

Commit to the Discomfort

Making room for new stories about race and engaging in conversations about racism can be a messy endeavor. Even with my experience—growing up with a limited awareness of race, beginning to unearth my racial bias in college, and then pastoring multi-racial churches—I still feel the tension surrounding the topics of race and racism. I still feel uncomfortable talking with my closest friends about racism. The conversations about race that I have with church leaders are full of misunderstanding too. We all know we carry these single stories, and we are afraid of saying the wrong thing. Yet, I encourage you to embrace this discomfort. Even if the conversation does not end with tidy answers, keep learning. Keep talking.

Talking about racism can be extraordinarily difficult in church. We like to assume that because we're Christian, we love each other well; we like to assume that, as followers of Christ, we do not reflect or foster racist beliefs. Austin Channing Brown challenges these assumptions in

her memoir *I'm Still Here: Black Dignity in a World Made for Whiteness.*
Brown writes, "At my Christian elementary school, we sang, 'Jesus loves
the little children . . . red and yellow, black and white, all are precious in
his sight.'" Yet, she continues, "I learned pretty early in life that while
Jesus may be cool with racial diversity, America is not. The ideology that
whiteness is supreme, better, best, permeates the air we breathe—in our
schools, in our offices, and in our country's common life."[7] Yes, Brown
argues, systemic racism is present in the everyday lives of Christians.

Yes, racism is present in our lives and in the churches we attend. For
white persons who are members of the majority culture in the United
States, it may be difficult for us to see how racism has grown in the
nooks and crannies of our churches and church life. We either can't see
it or have gotten good at overlooking it. It looks like organizing mission trips for all-white youth groups to serve in communities of color
without asking why these communities are impoverished in the first
place. It looks like feeding the homeless without wondering why there
are so many people of color in shelters. It looks like inviting only people
who look like us to serve as the leaders of our churches and denominations. Unearthing racial bias in the foundational elements of our Christian upbringing is not easy. More than once, I have felt ashamed. Since
reading Brown's book, I've found myself wondering again how I want
to talk about race with my daughter in a Christian context and how I
want to discuss it with my congregation. Acknowledging that persons
of color do not have the privilege of avoiding these conversations, brave
churches are called to step into the discomfort, creating space for admit-
ting mistakes we've made and for considering the changes we want to
make in our faith communities.

Confronting racism requires hard work. And we find the courage to
do that hard work when we see, hear, and learn how painful it is for our
Black and Brown siblings to experience and live with racism every day.
These tough conversations can be similar to the massive church work-
days where you pull every old thing out of the closets and cabinets, dust
it off, and decide what is life-giving for the entire community and what
needs to go. When you start talking about racism, your congregation
might decide they need to dust off and reconsider a beloved chapter

of church history. Or reexamine the weekly prayer practices that feel essential to who you are. Or readjust the church budget to afford new racial justice causes. These decisions and changes can come with pain. Even with commitment and careful planning, you likely will face the temptation to throw up your hands and say, "Why are we doing this? It's too hard!" But with time and attention, you can name the prejudice, bias, and misconceptions in your story.

BRAVE CHURCH

No justice. No peace. Cries for racial justice sounded across the globe in the aftermath of George Floyd's death. Despite the COVID-19 pandemic, people of all races joined in protest and flooded the streets first in Minneapolis and then in cities and towns across the United States and the world. Many churches started asking what they could do to combat racism. I received emails from church members I would have never expected to ask me this question: "When are we going to protest?" On June 7, 2020, we held aloft signs that read, "Black Lives Matter" and marched in the first protest in our neighborhood, a white suburb of Washington, DC. We felt good about our actions; our sister churches of color said, "It's about time." As congregations continue to look for new ways to confront racism, we can look to the example set by the brave churches who have been doing this difficult work for years.

Broadneck Baptist Church in Annapolis, Maryland

The death of Freddie Gray in 2015 captured the attention of Broadneck Baptist Church. The twenty-five-year-old Black man was arrested for possession of a switchblade in Baltimore. Forty-five minutes after his arrest, he was found unconscious in a police transport van. Gray died a week later. Riots erupted in Baltimore after the release of video footage from the arrest that showed Gray screaming in pain while two white officers held him to the ground. Criminal charges were brought against the officers who were later acquitted. The trauma of these events sparked new conversations about racism at Broadneck, a church located about forty-five minutes from Baltimore.

In a neighborhood of mostly white churches, Broadneck's racial diversity positioned the church as a leader for community conversations and reconciliation. Gray's death made those conversations seem all the more urgent to Rev. Abby Thornton Hailey. When she looked at photos of Gray, she saw the black- and brown-skinned boys who would soon come of age in her church. "When I began to think [about] how easily one of these boys we know and love could become the next Freddie Gray, another life lost to violence or to the depths of the prison system, I felt we as a congregation could not afford to be silent on matters of racial justice any longer," Hailey said. "Our kids' lives literally depend on it."[8] Confronting racism, naming it as a sin, became a personal and pastoral mission for Hailey.

Facilitating conversations about racism would become a cornerstone of Broadneck's social ministry. The church started with small focused events—a screening of the film *Selma* (2015) and a trip to an African American history museum—designed to build trust among church members. Then, the Broadneck invited members of the neighborhood and of other area churches to watch the PBS documentary series "The African Americans: Many Rivers to Cross." Broadneck hoped twenty or thirty folks would come to the three-part program. To the congregation's surprise, over eighty people arrived each night to watch and discuss the documentary. Of course, these first community conversations about racism had their awkward moments. Hailey recalled that not everyone came with the intention of listening with an open mind: Some folks wanted to talk only about themselves; others asked invasive questions of people they had just met. Still, Hailey said, "People kept showing up and listening to each other."[9] So the church kept hosting conversations about race each month.

Floyd's tragic death brought new life into these conversations. While the topics of systemic racism and police violence were not new, attendance for these now online discussions doubled in the summer of 2020. Broadneck also decided to organize its first protest. "A Black Lives

Matter protest in our neighborhood would have been unimaginable not long ago," Hailey said. "It was long overdue."[10] Breaking the pattern of silence in suburbs, parishioners gathered on June 17 to mark the fifth anniversary of the Emmanuel AME massacre. Parishioners stood along the street in front of the church holding signs that denounced racial injustice and affirmed Black Lives Matter. For churches who have been inspired to start talking about racism, Hailey offered some advice. "Be in it for the long haul. Our country's racial history has so many layers; they will not be peeled away easily," she said. "Be prepared for people to leave the conversation because it's just too hard. And try to have a racially diverse group with the white folks ready to listen."[11] Hailey said the more diverse the crowd is, the richer the conversations can be.

Martin Luther King, Jr. Christian Church in Reston, Virginia

Rev. Dr. Jean Robinson-Casey also is called to the ministry of racial diversity and reconciliation. For the last fourteen years, she's pastored Martin Luther King, Jr. Christian Church. Founded in 1982, the church received special permission to use the civil rights legend's name from Coretta Scott King (Dr. King's wife). All people are welcome in this church that provides a place to worship and "to pass down the historical traditions of the African American history for generations to come."[12] Robinson-Casey seeks to make King Church, as the members call it, a space of deep belonging. Questions that flow from her leadership include: What does it mean to be Black in America? How does the Black experience form a Christian experience? How does the congregation move forward in love, no matter what? To many members of the predominately African American congregation, the church offers safety from the racial inequalities of their lives. But Robinson-Casey doesn't believe that safety encapsulates the fullness of the gospel.

Robinson-Casey asks her congregation to confront racism in all of its forms and to extend that feeling of deep belonging to everyone who walks through the church doors. "People often talk about racism between Blacks and whites, but there's racism everywhere," she said.[13] She presses Black members of her congregation to examine the relationship they have with their Latinx neighbors. "We're all fighting for the same crumbs at the bottom," she explained. "The way we treat one another often times shows our racism. Neither of us wants the other to get ahead."[14] When Robinson-Casey began her pastorate, she learned that King Church shared its building with a Centro Christiano Ad El Shaddai, a Pentecostal congregation with members from Honduras and Guatemala. She observed that the two congregations knew of each other, but that's where their connection stopped. Robinson-Casey brought the two congregations together for a worship service—now an annual tradition. The joint service is led by both pastors and both choirs, and both congregations prepare food for shared meal. While language barriers can make extensive conversations difficult, the gatherings are "a little piece of heaven," Robinson-Casey said. "We see love in one another's eyes, and it means something."[15] She hopes that one day the two churches will share resources as well as educational and employment opportunities with one another.

As King Church works to confront its own prejudices, it mourns and protests the racism leveled at the African American community. In the summer of 2020, Robinson-Casey said, "we realized that we were dealing with two pandemics: not only COVID-19 but racism too."[16] In the face of Floyd's death, the congregation felt called to action. They also felt great fear; some members worried that taking steps of protest could make the church a target for racial violence. Still, they bravely moved forward with their plans. They unfurled a Black Lives Matter banner in front of their building. They started talking about racism with other churches. And they invited local faith communities to join them in August for a car rally for racial justice. "It was an awesome day of feeling supported as a community with so many people of faith standing with us," Robinson-Casey said.[17] The rally drew over two hundred cars and brought together ten congregations, including *Centro Christiano*, a Jewish synagogue, and an Islamic mosque.

In efforts to confront racism, both King Church and Broadneck Baptist began with small but persistent steps. These brave churches point to the wisdom of taking cues from your community, allotting ample time for discussion, and celebrating every victory. Don't wait for someone else to initiate the conversation. It's time to start talking about racism.

BRAVE TALK

1. What do you remember about your earliest experience of race? When you were growing up, how did your family talk about race? How did you talk about racism?
2. How do you define *racism*? When you have talked about racism at home or at church, what disagreements have you had? What are the sources of conflict in these conversations? How can the teachings of Jesus inform your approach to these conversations?
3. What are the "single stories" you've been told about people of other races and cultures? What stereotypes do you hold? How can you make room for new stories?
4. As you reflect on the ministries of Broadneck Baptist Church and Martin Luther King, Jr. Christian Church, what ideas resonate with you? What seems most brave about the way each church talks about racism?
5. How do you plan to continue talking about racism at church and at home? How can you confront racism in your everyday life?

BRAVE ACT

Review the list of resources for this chapter. Commit to continuing the conversation you started today by reading one of these books or engaging in a longer study using one of these guides. Make brave conversations about race and racism a central part of your spiritual formation.

CHAPTER 6

Let's Talk About Sexuality

Then God said, "Let us make humankind in our image, according to our likeness; and let them have dominion over the fish of the sea, and over the birds of the air, and over the cattle, and over all the wild animals of the earth, and over every creeping thing that creeps upon the earth." So, God created humankind in his image, in the image of God he created them.

—GENESIS 1:26-27

Have you ever felt like you were not welcome in church? Have you ever thought that God might love you less because of some central part of your identity? Or have you thought that your interpretation of the Bible was unpermitted or devalued by your faith community? Questions like these are at the heart of our conversation in this chapter. Sexual orientation and gender identity are deeply polarizing topics for the church. Conversations about sexuality often elicit strong feelings, a multitude of personal stories, differing takes on church history, and opposing beliefs about doctrine. In an effort to keep the peace, we often agree to disagree about sexuality. We fear that when we start talking, conflict might escalate quickly from respectful disagreements to hurtful accusations.

Yet, the storyteller in Genesis offers us an invitation to slow down and begin again. "In the beginning God created the heavens and the earth" (1:1, adapted). Day and night. Water and sea. The birds of the air. The fish of the sea. Every living thing. Then, God created human-kind. We're told that we're different from the rest of creation: We are made in the image of God. Not just some of us but all of us. God loves each one of us so much that God's own likeness makes an imprint on our entire being—body, mind, and spirit.[1] As children of God, we share this likeness. Sit with that for a minute.

We *all* are made in the image of God. How might this belief shape your conversation about sexual orientation and gender identity? How might it help you to see one another with love? As you gather for con-versation, take notice of each person who is present in your group. Turn and look your neighbor in the eye and say, "You are made in the image of God," or as the popular saying goes, "The God in me sees the God in you." Then, ask one person to lead this body prayer for the rest of the group:

God who made the heavens (reach toward the sky)
God who made the earth below (reach toward your toes)
God who made me (hands to heart)
And my neighbors near and far (stretch to the right, stretch to the left)
Help me to know that it is your light (reach toward the sky)
And it is your peace (reach toward your toes)
That ground me (hands to heart)
In this community (stretch to the right, stretch to the left)
Amen (hands folded together).

BRAVE EXPLORATION

People around the world disagree on the topic of sexuality. The lack of global consensus is reflected in national laws for same-sex relationships and gender expression. Out of the almost two hundred countries in the world, seventy countries criminalize same-sex relations and punish people who openly identify as lesbian, gay, bisexual, transgender, or queer (LGBTQ). Twenty-six of those nations penalize offenders with prison sentences ranging from ten years to life, and seven impose the death penalty.[2] In contrast, twenty-nine countries have legalized same-sex marriage. The United States joined that number after a 2015 United States Supreme Court ruling; the 5–4 decision in Obergefell v. Hodges gave same-sex couples a constitutional right to wed.[3]

Despite the legal framework for same-sex marriage in the United States, public support is far from unanimous, particularly among Christian Americans. According to Pew Research Center data, the number of Americans who favor allowing same-sex marriage increased from 37 percent in 2009 to 62 percent in 2017. But then, the numbers leveled off; in 2019, six in ten Americans supported same-sex marriage.[4] The data from 2019 also reveals demographic divides by religious affiliation and Christian denominations. Almost 80 percent of Americans who are religiously unaffiliated favor same-sex marriage. In contrast, 66 percent of white mainline Protestants, 61 percent of Catholics, and 29 percent of white evangelical Protestants supported same-sex marriage in 2019.[5]

The Christian Divide on Sexuality

These numbers likely reflect what you already know: Christians remain divided—and with great conviction—on the topic of sexual orientation and gender identity. Scan any Christian Living section at a big-box bookstore, and you'll find titles reflecting a pro-LGBTQ perspective on scriptures as well as authors who believe marriage outside of one man and one woman is an abomination. In your own community, I imagine you know some Jesus-loving people who believe we should "hate the sin, love the sinner." I bet you also know some Jesus-loving people who believe that gender is fluid and that marriage need not be restricted to a man and a woman.

These disagreements are not entirely new. The ethics of sexuality have been debated since the earliest days of Christianity, according to Rev. William B. Lawrence of Perkins School of Theology at Southern Methodist University. Since the third century, Christians have been using their stance on sexuality to distinguish themselves from those outside the faith. Lawrence observes that Christians often "find a single issue and use that as the red line that says you're either on one side of this or the other."[6] Slavery, temperance, conscientious objection to war, and abortion have also acted as single dividing issues. Sexuality, Lawrence notes, is different because it raises a question of identity rather than behavior. It also demands decisive action from churches. Pastors can choose to talk about abortion during a sermon or dodge the issue altogether. But with sexuality, churches have to decide: Will you perform a same-sex marriage? Will you ordain a person who identifies as LGBTQ?

These decisions have widened the rifts between churches and have fractured denominations. After decades of in-fighting, the Presbyterian Church (USA) opted to sanction same-sex marriages in 2015 and spurred a small exodus of more conservative parishioners from the denomination. When the Episcopal Church of the United States of America updated its definition of marriage in 2015 and voted to allow clergy to perform same-sex weddings, the decision distressed the wider Anglican community and drew criticism from the Archbishop in England. Many of the Episcopalians who left in protest joined the Anglican Church of North America, a denomination founded in 2009 by traditionalists who believed ECUSA had become too liberal.[7] The United Methodist Church will face the same decision in 2022 about whether to split over the issue of same-sex marriage and the ordination of LGBTQ pastors.[8]

With these deep divisions, faith-based organizations struggle to represent the values of the church. World Vision, a Christian humanitarian organization, made headlines for changing its hiring policies. In 2014, the nonprofit announced it would hire Christians in same-sex relationships. The announcement garnered praise from some Christians, who saw the decision as a win for gay rights, and intense criticism from others, who saw the change as a disavowal of biblical authority. Within forty-eight hours, World Vision reversed its stance and reverted to its original hiring policies.[9] The organization's flip-flop illustrates our irresolution about what we collectively believe.

How Do We Stay in Conversation?

When we debate same-sex relationships within our faith communities, our conversations typically circle around to scripture. "What does the Bible say about sexuality?" someone invariably asks. Then, we may read and reread texts that speak of it directly. Christians who do not affirm same-sex relationships point to six scriptures as proof of the sin: Genesis 19:1-10; Leviticus 18:22, 201:13; Romans 1:26-27; 1 Corinthians 6:9; and 1 Timothy 1:9-10. Christians who affirm same-sex relationships offer a contextual interpretation of these texts and muse about the silence on the topic in other parts of the Bible (such as from the words of Jesus). Churches include their beliefs about sexuality in public statements of faith and in the information that they provide on their websites. A church's stance on same-sex marriage may be a deciding factor when we choose where we want to attend services.

We've let our beliefs about sexuality divide our families and separate us from people we once called friends. As a pastor, I've listened to countless parishioners share how they can no longer spend time with certain friends or family members because they are not in favor of gay marriage (or vice versa). Some of these relationships may be untenable; I certainly am not advocating for LGBTQ persons to put themselves into unsafe situations. But so often we stop talking to people because we disagree with their perspectives. When we let our differences isolate us, we can forget that we previously enjoyed golfing with Uncle Tim in the summer. Or trading parenting tips with Charlotte from high school. Or going to neighborhood yoga with Mary Beth. Do we really mean to end these relationships altogether?

We can keep talking. In this conversation about sexuality, as with all of the other brave conversations, the goal is not to convince people of our beliefs or change anyone's mind about the topic. It's not the time for proof-texting scripture or for debating theological interpretations of the Bible. Rather, the purpose of this session is simply to listen—even if we might feel a little uncomfortable—for as long as we are able to do this brave work. I believe it is possible to keep talking about sexual orientation and gender identity with fellow Christians, even those with whom we disagree, if we can cultivate affection for one another and listen with compassion.

Cultivate Affection for One Another

Affection acts as the glue that holds relationships together. In *The Four Loves*, C. S. Lewis explores four Greek verbs that are used to describe love in the New Testament: *storge* (affection), *philia* (friendship), *eros* (romantic love), and *agape* (God's love). For *storge*, the least studied type of love, Lewis provides only one criterion: "Its objects have to be familiar."[10] Think, for example, about people you see frequently but don't consider your friends: the crossing guard at your child's school, the postman who delivers your mail, or a member of your once-a-month bridge club. These people may be quite different from you; yet, through frequent interaction, you may have developed an affection for one another—a fondness between human beings in a shared community.

Here's the beauty of *storge*: This love can bring together people who lack common cultural denominators (age, race, sex, class, or education) and even people with opposing worldviews. Affection "can unite those who most emphatically, even comically, are not [made for one another]: people who, if they had not found themselves put down by fate in the same household or community, would have had nothing to do with each other."[11] Consider, for a moment, your congregation or even the members of your study group. You might have little else in common, but you share the same house of worship. You see one another every Sunday, and you share memories of the same events. You likely have developed an affection for one another.

Cultivating *storge* is not passive work. Affection "grows out of the regular routines of shared life, short conversations, exchanged pleasantries, and proffered gratuities," explains Scott Bader-Saye, a professor at Seminary of the Southwest. He believes that developing affection requires "a deep commitment to presence."[12] This commitment might mean talking with the clerk at the grocery store, giving into laughter during a family game night, or thanking your child's teacher after a tense parent conference. Or in a church setting, it might mean passing candy to your pew-mate or listening to a story told by someone whose voice grates on you. These small gestures help to remind you that, even though you see the world differently, you can still appreciate one another.

The work of cultivating affection pays off during the tough conversations. The mutual appreciation that is developed over time can help keep us together—even when we disagree about a topic. "Focusing on affection helps us to have realistic expectations," Bader-Saye writes. "We may never really like everyone in the pews around us, but we can strive to notice, endure, smile, and even appreciate them."[13] Loving our neighbors doesn't mean we have to agree with their opinions or support their choices; even if we don't count all our fellow church members as our friends, we can share with them the love of affection—*storge*. Leaning into the affection we have for one another can help us to stay in the hard conversations.

Listen with Compassion

Deepening our compassion also can help us to navigate tough conversations. As we wrestle with scripture on the topic of sexuality, we often start drafting doctrine and stop seeing, hearing, and loving people. In his book *God and the Gay Christian: The Biblical Case in Support of Same-Sex Relationships*, Matthew Vines writes about his experience of coming out to his church family. "Homosexuality, to the limited extent it was discussed in our church, was little more than a political football, a quick test of orthodoxy," Vines recalls. "In all of this, the concerns, lives and dignity of gay *people* were not mentioned."[14] In his account, coming out led to social isolation, discrimination, and loss of friends and family support.

Vines's story echoes the experience of many LGBTQ persons. Statistics tell us that 40 percent of people who identify as LGBTQ have been rejected by a family member or close friend because of their sexual orientation or gender identity. About 30 percent have experienced overt expressions of unwelcome in their houses of worship.[15] Preston Sprinkle, the author of *People to Be Loved: Why Homosexuality Is Not Just an Issue,* describes how people who identify as LGBTQ often are scared of going church; they worry they might "be harassed or harmed, beat up or bullied—verbally or physically—if they stepped across the holy threshold on Sunday."[16] While such abuse may not be realized, the church experience for LGBTQ persons is often one of fear. To help us consider perspectives from the LGBTQ community in our conversation, I want to share two stories that encapsulate the stories I've heard as a pastor.

Robert, who identifies as gay, soon will be married to his partner of five years. When he was growing up, Robert's grandmother took him to church every Sunday. He sang solos in the annual Christmas pageants. He fondly remembers youth group beach trips and lock-ins in the church social hall—until he began to talk about his sexuality. Then, his youth minister told him he couldn't go on any more trips unless he agreed to separate lodging. When his pastor slipped him pamphlets on reparative therapy, Robert slipped out the church doors and never came back. He still believes in God, but he no longer seeks membership in a community where he would be an unwanted outsider.

Becky also grew up in the church. Becky identifies as transgender; she was born male but now identifies as female. She remembers a congregation that nurtured her, supported her, and even presented her with a college scholarship when she graduated from high school. Everyone believed that she would thrive in church leadership—until word got around that she wasn't Bart anymore but Becky. The church council revoked her scholarship and asked her to not wear what they described as "drag" clothes to worship. Taunted all over town, even by her former Sunday school teacher, Becky was devastated. Now she does not want to be a part of any community that doesn't respectfully use her pronouns of she/her/hers.

While Robert and Becky cannot represent the experiences of everyone who identifies as LGBTQ, sadly, these stories are not unusual. Not all LGBTQ persons experience persecution, and some who have been hurt by their churches find their way into affirming faith communities. But more often, people leave the church and never come back. Matthew Vines clarifies here what is at stake: "This debate is not simply about beliefs and rights; it's about people who are created in God's image. Those people may be like you or entirely *un*like you."[17] We can create compassionate communities of faith when we remember our shared humanity and listen to one another's stories with respect and affection.

BRAVE CHURCH

Brave churches make room for the stories of people who identify as LGBTQ. Brave churches listen to the perspectives of all parishioners—those who believe that homosexuality is wrong and those who believe that the church should welcome and affirm same-sex relationships and a spectrum of gender expressions. Brave churches cultivate compassion and *storge*, leaning on these bonds when they start talking about sexuality. These two brave churches show us how.

Baptist Church of the Covenant in Birmingham, Alabama

The Baptist Church of the Covenant (BCOC) has been talking about tough topics since its founding in 1970. When a downtown Birmingham church refused a membership to a mother and daughter because they were Black, a group of parishioners walked out in protest and later formed the BCOC.[18] The church's history led to its defining mission of unconditional welcome, and the church's affirmed openness has attracted many members.

Pastor Emeritus Rev. Sarah Shelton recalls arriving in 2002 at a church that held an affiliation with the Southern Baptist Convention and maintained a membership that included many Christians who identified as LGBTQ. "I was so grateful that BCOC would call me as their pastor that I went determined to love and welcome all just as they were already doing," Shelton said. "As relationships grew, the stigma disappeared, and all of us were able to just see one another as fellow travelers on a faith journey."[19] The BCOC congregation found a way to hold affection for one another despite differing viewpoints among church members on the topic of sexuality.

The federal legalization of same-sex marriage tested those bonds. After hearing some concerns about the church performing weddings for gay couples, Shelton met with each church member who expressed dissenting views. She wanted all voices to be heard. She encouraged the congregation to love and care for one another, even if they had different perspectives.[20] Though the topic of same-sex weddings was openly discussed at a church gathering, the matter never came to a congregational vote. Bolstered by its strong relationships, the congregation agreed to keep the church's existing policies that were stated without reference to sexual identity; weddings could occur in the sacred space of the church for the purpose of making a spiritual covenant between God and the couple.[21] While church members still disagreed on the ethics of sexual orientation, they got through this potentially fracturing moment by prioritizing compassion and affection for one another.

St. Andrew's United Methodist Church in Orangeburg, South Carolina

Other churches have started talking more recently about sexuality. St. Andrew's United Methodist Church is a close-knit congregation whose members hold different views on sexual orientation, gender identity, and the church. Despite their differences, members wanted to be informed as the General Conference of The United Methodist Church continued to debate whether or not to affirm LGBTQ ordination and same-sex marriage. "We wanted people to talk with each other, not at or about each other," said Rev. Carol Cannon, so the church offered a four-week study during Lent of 2018. They used the Cokesbury guide *Living Faithfully: Human Sexuality and the United Methodist Church* that offers a balanced presentation of the traditionalist and progressive viewpoints. Together, church members examined the arguments made for and against same-sex relationships and the ways these viewpoints are supported by scripture, tradition, reason, and experience. Cannon attributes the study's success to the posture of the attendants: "Each person came to participate and learn, not simply to observe or to argue their own viewpoint."[22] St. Andrew's congregation models an example of how we can make room for disagreements and challenge ideas rather than people.

Both St. Andrew's and BCOC found ways to talk about sexuality. Their church leaders didn't avoid the topic; instead they structured time for intentional conversation. In facilitated discussions, church members held tension with one another, leaned on the loving bonds of affection, and listened with compassion to the experiences, feelings, and beliefs held by each member of the congregation. Even in the hard places of disagreement, these brave churches live in community with one another.

BRAVE TALK

1. Reread Genesis 1:1-27. Although you may have read this passage many times, what words or phrases stand out to you today? How might this scripture shape the way you approach conversations about sexuality in the future?
2. Describe a time when you disagreed with someone about church doctrine. What happened? How did you respond? How did the experience affect your relationship with that person?
3. Describe a relationship you've built from affection (*storge*). How did that affection come to be? How has that affection kept you in that relationship despite differences or tension between you?
4. Consider the examples of Baptist Church of the Covenant and St. Andrew's United Methodist Church. What stands out to you

about the ways these churches have approached conversations about sexuality?

5. How have you approached conversations in the past about sexual orientation and gender identity? How might you approach them differently in the future?

BRAVE ACT

Host a holiday gathering for Thanksgiving, Christmas, or Easter at your church or at someone's home. Invite people who might be left out of their family celebrations. Include members of the LGBTQ community. Commit to no agenda other than eating together. This meal can be an expression of Christian love and an opportunity to form new relationships.[23]

CHAPTER 7

Let's Keep Talking

"I truly understand that God shows no partiality, but in every nation anyone who fears him and does what is right is acceptable to him."

—ACTS 10:34-35

*A*s you begin this last chapter, what do you notice about yourself? Think about how you entered conversations at the beginning of this study. How will you approach the conversation your group has this week? How have you changed? Over the course of this study, you have shared your perspectives and experiences related to the tough topics of infertility and miscarriage, mental illness, domestic violence, racism, and sexuality. You have listened with intention to your group members, and you have owned the impact of your contributions to the conversation. I imagine you are in a different headspace than you were seven weeks ago.

While you might not have changed your mind about any topic, your mindset may have changed. The goal of the study was to change not *what* you think but rather *how* you engage in conversations with people who may disagree with you. You've opened your heart to this hard work. You've asked new questions of yourself, of the people around you, and of your church. You've taken risks—allowing yourself to be vulnerable and staying present even as you felt tension rise in the room. You have become a more courageous congregation. I hope this study is only the beginning for your brave church.

The story of Peter in Acts 10 encourages us to continue this work. One of the twelve disciples and a lifelong Jew, Peter receives a vision that shows him, " 'What God has made clean, you must not call profane' " (Acts 10:15). He is shocked to learn that, as a Christian, he's no longer bound to follow every rule of law. Right away, the Holy Spirit nudges Peter to welcome into his home a Gentile and Roman centurion named Cornelius. What a scandal! Jews did not hang out, much less share lodging, with Gentiles; Roman centurions did not enter the homes of people under their supervision. Peter and Cornelius were unlikely friends. Yet, through their exchange—this taboo conversation—Cornelius hears the good news of Jesus for the first time, and Peter comes to understand "that God shows no partiality." Without opening their minds, listening to God, and listening to each other, the two men would have missed a beautiful experience of God's presence in the world. They needed each other.

As you gather for your last meeting, consider the gifts you have received during this study. Invite each group member to offer a word or phrase in response to this question: *How have you experienced God's love during these brave conversations?* Pause in silence for a moment after each person's response to honor the words that have been shared. Then, ask one group member to share aloud this invocation:

God, none of us could have imagined where this journey of faith would take us. As these sessions come to an end, we give thanks to you, Surprising One. For the gift of seeing anew our traveling companions. For moments of connection. For the experience of listening and then listening some more to people we don't always understand. For fresh perspectives and insights. For unlikely friendships. God, you have brought forth new things in us. We've asked new questions of ourselves and of our church. As we look to what might be ahead, we thank you for already preparing a way. Amen.

BRAVE EXPLORATION

I have a friend, Susan, who used to travel regularly from the United States to India for humanitarian work. One day I asked her how she could bear those long flights. "If air travel sped up," I mused, "we could hop between continents in less than a day. Wouldn't that be so much better?"

"Oh, I would hate that," she replied.

"Why?" I wanted to know. I didn't believe that anyone actually enjoyed eating airplane food or sleeping in cramped quarters.

"Because I think when you go from one land to another, you need a pause—some time to be not where you were but not yet where you're going. If I can, I like taking a daylong layover somewhere in between to ground myself, to remember who I am, and to think about how my recent experiences have changed me."

I have been grateful for the wisdom of her practice during times of transition in my own life, and I offer it to you now to use during the last session of *Brave Church*. For as we reach the end of this study, we are neither where we used to be nor yet where we are going. Let's claim this liminal moment—this in-between space—for all its unique offerings. Take some time with your group to remember who you are, to consider how this study has changed you (individually and as a congregation), and to explore ways you can build on the momentum these conversations have created. As you relish in this pause, I offer you two practices that may give you a way forward: listen to new people and listen to more stories.

Listen to New People

We rarely give much thought to who we include in (or exclude from) our conversations. I recently led a church retreat where I gave each participant a picture of a dinner table with blank name cards at each of the eight place settings. I asked the participants to imagine the table was prepared for a party they hosted at their home or for a meetup they organized at a restaurant. Who would be there? After everyone slotted names, I invited them to share a brief description. Were the people at the table family members? Were they neighbors, children's friends, or work colleagues? Was the group racially or economically diverse? Did one person stick out as unlike the others? Many participants described restaurant gatherings. ("I don't like to have people over to see my mess!") And they almost all described tables filled with family or close friends. In most cases, the people at the table belonged to the same racial and socioeconomic group as the host. "We talk a good game around here about diversity being important to our Christian faith," one woman reflected. "But when I thought about who I spend my time with, these folks looked a lot like me." If we're honest, most of us would say the same.

Without thinking about it, we gravitate toward people of similar racial and economic backgrounds; we tend to prefer the company of people who have had similar life experiences and who likely share our opinions and beliefs. I don't know anyone who wakes up and thinks, *I want to talk with someone who adamantly disagrees with me today. That sounds fun!* However, as I hope we've all discovered during this study, these difficult conversations are so important. When we are committed to talking with people outside of our regular social circles, we open ourselves to seeing the world in a new way. We have an opportunity to explore fresh ideas and to build relationships. As our tables fill with new faces, our capacity for welcome expands, and we begin to create the kind of community that Christ calls us to create.

Listen to More Stories

When I check in with my husband at the end of the day, I ask simple questions: "How was your day?" or "Did your meeting go well?" He responds to my questions not with simple one-sentence answers but with elaborate tales. He knows no other way to relay information than through storytelling. When I first met Kevin, I worried that his long stories would hinder my let's-get-on-with-things approach to life. But the longer we've been together, the more I've come to value his gift. Kevin's stories allow me to learn about his days as he wants me to hear about them. He feels heard as I listen, and we laugh a lot in the process.

If I received the CliffsNotes version of his day instead of taking in the entirety of his tale, the strength of our relationship would decline. Kevin's stories help me to know him better.

Storytelling is a vehicle for connection in congregational life too. As theologians Vaughan S. Roberts and David Sims write in *Leading by Story: Rethinking Church Leadership*, "Stories do not just reflect togetherness; they also produce it. Listening to stories together is an ancient human form of fellowship."[1] Stories can help us to understand and to develop an appreciation for people—even for people who hold beliefs that oppose our own. A few examples: You might believe that terminating a pregnancy is immoral; yet, when you hear a woman talking about the circumstances that led her to such a momentous decision, you convey respect by listening. You may believe that America needs tougher gun control laws; yet, when you listen to the reasons your neighbor is a proud gun owner, you open your mind to validity of another point of view.[2] Or, more practically, you might not think that your church needs to replace the carpet in the sanctuary this year; yet, when you take into consideration the wishes of the people who do, you create space for living together with difference.

BRAVE CHURCH

We value people by valuing their stories. By listening to more stories and listening to people who have life experiences and beliefs that differ from our own, we cultivate a sense of shared humanity. As Peter learns from his experience with Cornelius, Christ ushers in new ways of being in relationship with one another. As Christians, we are called to tear down the barriers between us, to choose unlikely conversation partners, and to listen with open hearts to the stories of all the people we encounter. This section highlights two churches and a nonprofit organization that are breaking down barriers and building up community.

Braver Angels @ Lewinsville Presbyterian Church in McLean, Virginia

Politics and church—the two usually don't mix well. In the past two decades, American politics has become increasingly polarized. Our disagreements have led to distrust and contempt for the "other side." Some research indicates that our nation is now almost as polarized as it was during the Civil War.[3] As the political landscape grows increasingly tense, churches struggle to discern if and how they should respond. Rev. Dr. Scott Ramsey, a senior pastor at Lewinsville Presbyterian Church, said his church has been wrestling with tough questions, like this one: "Is our goal to move in a particular direction, or is it to keep people together?"[4] Politics are inescapable for Lewinsville, which is located about twenty minutes from Washington, DC.

To help make "important conversations happen" in the community,[5] the church has opened its doors and offered its space to Braver Angels, a nonprofit committed to reducing political polarization and seeking common ground among Americans. Shortly after the 2016 election, the founders brought together ten Trump supporters and eleven Clinton supporters in Ohio for its first Red/Blue Workshop. The pilot workshop tested whether people with opposing political views could still listen to one another, disagree respectfully, and come together as Americans. The answer was yes. News of the workshop's success spread, and a national nonprofit was born.[6] Ramsey said his church began hosting Braver Angels because the workshops "validate the experience of all participants" and allow them to "see the Venn diagram overlap of ideas that we can so easily overlook right now."[7] For Lewinsville Presbyterian, Braver Angels acts as a tool to bridge divides in their community of faith.

In the summer of 2019, I observed an all-day Red/Blue workshop at Lewinsville Presbyterian and took notes on the dialogue that occurred between five Republicans ("reds") and five Democrats ("blues"). After introducing some rules similar to those we discussed in chapter 1, the two facilitators separated the reds and blues and asked them to identify the stereotypes that other side had about them. For example, the blues said the reds believed they "hated America," "wanted to kill babies," and "thought government was an answer to everything." Meanwhile, the reds said the blues thought they were "racist," "sexist," and "anti-immigration." The facilitators confronted each group this follow-up question: "What is the kernel of truth in the stereotype?" When the reds and blues meet together, they shared their lists of stereotypes and then answered two more questions: "What did you learn about how the other side sees themselves?" and "What do you have in common with the other side?" Bravely, the reds and blues stayed committed to the process. No one left. And when asked to find common ground, participants responded with answers like these: "I see how we want similar things but just have a different approach to get there" and "It's hard to hate people up close." The conversation did not change anyone's political beliefs, but it changed the way people thought about one another.

Lewinsville is not the only church who has welcomed Braver Angels. The workshops are especially important for faith communities, said Mel Pine, the Braver Angels coordinator for Virginia. The goal, Pine explains, "is not to turn people into political moderates; it's to help them remember that they are not enemies because their beliefs differ."[8] A practicing Buddhist who grew up in a Jewish family, Pine frequently meets for coffee with a Southern Baptist he met through Braver Angels.[9] If we bring a genuine curiosity about other people's experiences, Pine believes any conversation can be an opportunity to learn and to extend God's love. Braver Angels is "about people seeing the holy in themselves and in others," Pine said. "It does seem to me like a spiritual practice."[10] Another woman who was observing the workshop with me echoed this sentiment, exclaiming, "I'm so glad I'm here. This is what church ought to be about." Operating outside of the realm of faith, Braver Angels aims to bring people together as Americans. The organization's methods show us ways we can come together as Christians.

Gilead Church in Chicago, Illinois

Storytelling is a spiritual practice for Gilead Church in Chicago. Gilead was founded in 2016 by Rev. Rebecca Anderson (Disciples of Christ) and Rev. Vince Amlin (United Church of Christ). Worship at Gilead includes many traditional elements, like singing, praying, and sharing Communion. But each service also features three stories: two from members of the community and a third from a pastor who preaches in a storytelling style. The personal stories told at Gilead don't follow the form one might expect at church. Rather than "I once was lost and now I am found," Anderson said, "there are lots of stories that are 'I once was lost, and I'm still kind of a mess.'"[11] While few take the shape of traditional testimony, all of the stories are true.

No story is taboo at Gilead. There's no story too sad or too small or too controversial or too ordinary. As long as your story is true, you can tell it. Amlin said he encourages storytellers to avoid lecturing or preaching and instead to stay in the moment of their first-person narratives. He believes God is at work in these stories: "People have told very dramatic stories about getting arrested, getting hit by cars, falling in love, [witnessing] a traumatic death. People share turning points when their lives changed. But they also share very small stories that can be just as powerful. The drama of a week at summer camp when they were twelve. An episode of sleepwalking. A conflict at work."[12] Gilead hopes to convey that God values ordinary people and their everyday lives.

God dwells in our real lives. God is present in our celebration and our suffering, our tiny triumphs and our colossal mistakes, our big adventures and our daily grind. What makes even the simplest story beautiful, Rev. Amlin believes, is "the way people make meaning of the day to day."[13] Authentic storytelling makes meaningful connections possible. "It's one thing to know you are not the only one to have had a miscarriage," Anderson explained. "It's another thing to know someone else in the room who had a miscarriage."[14] You do not have to be a member of the church to tell a story at Gilead. The pastors recruit storytellers both from their congregation and from a storytelling group they host in the neighborhood.[15]

Sharing stories can connect a community; it can also connect a community to God. Storytelling gives Gilead new ways to hear the good news. For instance, consider Easter—a story central to the Christian faith and a day of pageantry for most churches. Christ is risen! Christ is risen indeed! At Gilead, Easter includes stories about resurrection *and* stories about darkness, disillusionment, and confusion—the tombs of our lives. Not all of the stories have happy endings. Sharing these stories gives the congregation a fresh perspective on the Easter story: Sometimes resurrection takes time.

Gilead's bold approach invites us to consider how we might listen to more stories at church. Some faith communities might host an open mic night or a storytelling circle. Other churches might give study groups permission to take a break and to spend time hearing and telling stories that matter to members. Church leaders might organize talkback sessions after worship services and give parishioners an opportunity to share stories that relate to that Sunday's themes. Pastors might offer personal stories connected to the message or sermon they gave. While each congregation's style will be unique, we all can find ways to bring storytelling into our spiritual practices.

Friends, while you may have completed *Brave Church*, your work has just begun. In you, God is birthing a beautiful new chapter of listening, learning, and sharing the good news. Yet, as you commit to becoming a brave church, your congregation may face tension that feels insurmountable. Your church or denomination might split (or split again). Your most inclusive welcome might offend. Take heart! Don't give up. The God of peace is with you. You are building the kind of beloved community that Jesus shows us how to create. Step by step, conversation by conversation, year by year—you'll be delightfully surprised at how good bravery feels.

BRAVE TALK

1. Review the conversations your group had about tough topics: infertility and miscarriage, mental illness, domestic violence, racism, and sexuality. Which conversation surprised you the most? Why?
2. How do you plan to keep talking with your congregation this year? Which topic from this study would you like to spend more time exploring? What other topics would you like to address as a congregation?
3. Describe a moment in your discussions when you needed to (a) bite your tongue, (b) ask a question, or (c) sit with the tension in the room. What was the outcome?
4. How might the Braver Angels model be used in a congregational setting? What aspects of the nonprofit organization's approach might benefit your church?
5. What's a memorable story you have heard recently? What details do you remember? What made the story memorable, moving, or relatable? How might this story be a "God story"? How might it help you to make a connection with the person who told it?

BRAVE ACT

Remember this study was only a beginner's guide. As your brave church looks for ways to continue the conversation, take a look at the resources for further conversations and check out at least one of the recommended articles, books, or websites. What brave conversation are you going to start next? Make a plan. Brave acts do not happen on their own.

LEADER'S GUIDE

*T*hank you for your willingness to be a brave leader. Your group is lucky to have you as a guide. In leading your small group through this book, you are offering a holy alternative to the divisiveness of our world. You are cultivating a community that seeks to listen to and to love one another well. You are showing that authentic conversations are possible in a faith community.

This guide is designed to help you lead a six-week study plus one optional bonus session. I encourage you to consider using this suggested format, but you may not have six weeks to spend studying this book with your community. Additionally, perhaps your community already has begun having conversations around some of the topics in this book. For example, maybe your church or small group recently completed an introductory anti-racism training or domestic violence awareness webinar and is ready for more than a beginner's look at either topic. That's not a problem. Skip those chapters, and plan your group sessions accordingly. Allow yourself and your group the flexibility to linger longer on topics that require more time.

As the leader of your group, you will want to review the sections in the introduction titled "Getting Started" and "How to Use This Book" before your first meeting. These sections will help you understand the intentions of the study and guidelines for group formation. Encourage group members to read the chapter for each week's session before the group meeting, if possible, and to think about the reflection questions under "Brave Talk" at the end of each chapter.

For those in your group who may feel overwhelmed at the thought of having brave conversations about tough topics, remind them of the observations I shared from the pilot study and the examples of churches and nonprofits from each chapter. My congregation was changed by our conversations. We observed Domestic Violence Awareness month for the first time in our history. Folks felt comfortable asking for prayer regarding mental health concerns that they previously had kept from other members of the congregation. We began talking about the racism present in our congregation and in our community. Tell participants that others have worked through these topics and thrived as a result. They can too!

My prayer for you as you begin is that you'll have the humility and the wisdom to come alongside all participants through whatever may come. I can't wait to hear more about your experience of *Brave Church*. If you would like to share your group's experience or if you have questions, please contact me through my website: elizabethhagan.com.

You've got this!

—Pastor Elizabeth

Session 1: Let's Talk

Preparation

Take time to familiarize yourself with the history and concept of safe and brave spaces. Consider what communities in your own life have been safe. Where have you experienced a brave space, if at all? Be prepared to share these experiences as relatable examples as you go over the concepts in the session. If you are meeting in person, make copies of the "Brave Space Covenant" found in appendix A for every group member.

Opening

As you gather your group for the first time, invite folks to take a few moments to breathe. Breathe in. Breathe out. Remind the participants that the Spirit of God is with them as they begin this journey. Invite each person in the group to name an intention for the time you will spend together that answers this question: What is your hope for the group experience?

Prayer

Ask one group member to offer this prayer: *Holy Spirit, as we begin this journey together, may we cease to be annoyed that others are not what we wish they were, since none of us is what we wish we were. Even in conflict, may we see people not as problematic but as beloved. Amen.*

Reading

Read Acts 2:1-12 aloud. Invite group members to share a word, phrase, or concept that stood out to them. What does this story teach about relationships? How might this scripture passage guide how your group becomes a community over the next six weeks? Ask participants to consider how they find themselves longing for authentic community.

Brave Talk

What about your current faith community feels safe? What feels brave? Consider writing a list or creating a chart of the brave space rules together. Post this list or chart in your physical or virtual meeting space. Invite group members to share which rules are familiar to them (or not) and how they have practiced them before in other settings. Emphasize that these rules will be the foundation of your conversations in this group. These guidelines will fuel your group's bravery and longevity. Reassure group members that no process like this is perfect. They will make mistakes, but in returning to the brave space rules, they will find their courage.

Closing

Review the "Brave Church Covenant" found in appendix A. Feel free to add to it or modify it with language that works better for your group. If meeting in person, invite all participants to sign one copy of the covenant that you will save and bring to each meeting. Remind group members that they will briefly review this covenant during each session as a reminder of their intention for their time together.

Session 2: Let's Talk About Infertility and Miscarriage

Preparation

Consider who you know who has struggled to conceive or birth a living child (maybe that person is you). If you have a close friend or family member who faced or is facing infertility or miscarriage, consider asking them if they would feel comfortable sharing more of their story of longing and loss with you. Practice compassionate listening by only asking clarifying questions if necessary. Ask them what they wish others knew about the experience of infertility and miscarriage, and thank them for sharing with you.

If you or someone you love have not experienced infertility and miscarriage, I invite you to read more about my own experience. I wrote a prayer of longing about my experience of infertility and miscarriage, which can be found here: https://elizabethhagan.com/prayer-grieving-mother/. How do these words prepare you as a leader to be sensitive to the experiences that might be shared in the group meeting? Be mindful of your role in the group meeting not to offer unsolicited advice but to listen and learn.

Opening

As you gather for conversation, begin with a moment of reflection after reviewing the "Brave Church Covenant." Invite participants to think about a time they were praying for something that they really wanted but did not receive. Ask group members to share a word or phrase that describes that unfulfilled longing.

Prayer

Ask one group member to offer this prayer: *God, we gather today not to run from pain but to come close to it. Give us the courage to offer our unfinished stories without sugarcoating them. Challenge us to see beyond our own experiences. Offer us peace for our wounds of loss that have not yet healed, and help us to be gentle with one another. Amen.*

Reading

Read 1 Samuel 1:1-11 aloud. Ask the group members to consider how Hannah's story is similar to or different from their own experiences of unfulfilled longing. How have they seen and heard Hannah's story taught or preached in ways that were unhelpful to those experiencing infertility and miscarriage? Pause to acknowledge the unseen or unknown pain present in your community.

Brave Talk

Review how your faith community normally celebrates or observes Mother's and Father's Day. With more information from this week's chapter about the history and intention of these days, how can your faith community alter (or not) those celebrations? How can your faith community as a whole and as individual members support those who are struggling with infertility and miscarriage?

Closing

Consider how you might connect with a ministry that serves children in foster care or without permanent families in your neighborhood or abroad. Ask the group if they would be interested in learning more about Orphan Sunday.

Session 3: Let's Talk About Mental Illness

Preparation

The phrase *mental illness* was chosen intentionally. This chapter deals with concerns that arise in persons and communities as a result of long-term, lifelong mental conditions. More than "feeling blue" or "needing a mental health day" (a phrase that we may commonly hear people use), this chapter addresses stigma and despair faced by those who experience chronic, medically supervised mental illness. Review the definition of *mental illness* and examples given in the "Brave Exploration" section of this chapter. Spend some time reflecting on your experiences with those suffering from mental illness. What is your own comfort level with this topic? Consider sharing any perceptions or biases that you have held with your small group.

Opening

Review the "Brave Church Covenant." Review the definition of *mental illness* found in the "Brave Exploration" section. Pause for few moments of silence. Encourage participants to consider how they can respectfully hold the stories they may hear in this time together.

Prayer

Ask one group member to offer this prayer: *God, we cry out to you with open hearts. We ask for the courage to share our pain—to tell stories that may be difficult to tell, to hear stories we might not want to hear, and to listen for the gifts our struggles can bring. We want to be a community that can sing sad songs. We want to be a community that does real life together. Amen.*

Reading

Read Psalm 88:3-8 aloud. Psalm 88 could be called "The Saddest Song in the Bible." We don't know much about the author, but we recognize the writer's ability to capture the anguish and isolation that often accompany mental illness. The psalmist seems withdrawn. We can imagine him crying out, "Where is my hope? Does my life matter?" What does the psalmist seem to long for? How might the psalmist's longings be similar to those of persons suffering from mental illness?

Brave Talk

One in five Americans will experience mental illness this year, yet the research shows us that the church doesn't like to talk about it. What keeps you from talking about mental illness? Consider the ministries of the Minnesota church as well as the one in North Carolina. What about their conversations and compassion ministries might be applicable to your setting?

Closing

Consider how you might pray for those struggling with mental illness—just as you pray for those who struggle with physical illness. How might you reshape the language you use in prayer in your community?

Session 4: Let's Talk About Domestic Violence

Preparation

Unique from other sections of the book, this chapter concerns theological concepts that may have shaped your responses to domestic violence as a Christian. Take some time to review each of the theological concepts before the group session. This session will require sensitivity to your own faith tradition and that of your group members. Often folks are raised in a tradition and arrive in adulthood in a completely different one. This might mean that while you or your church do not believe in a particular concept, some of the group members might still be shaped by their experiences from a childhood tradition. Be aware of this as you proceed through the material, and take time to check in with one another for clarification as needed.

Opening

After reviewing the "Brave Church Covenant," ask participants to consider their own experiences with domestic violence, either personal experiences or through relationships with a family member or friend. Open the floor to anyone who would like to share, reminding the group to be sensitive to the pain that might be brought to the surface because of this conversation. Emphasize that no one needs to feel pressured to share.

Prayer

Ask one group member to offer this prayer: *God, we never know what goes on behind closed doors. Soften our hearts as we consider the terror of*

this violence that is so often endured in secrecy. Deepen our empathy as we
hear stories that may seem unfathomable to us. Embolden us to speak up for
those who are afraid to speak up for themselves. Amen.

Reading

Read Psalm 55:4-6, 12-14 aloud. David describes an experience of fear
in Psalm 55. While we do not know the particularities of his situation,
we can gather from his writing that David is afraid of someone he used
to trust. People who experience domestic violence today feel this same
terror, shock, and betrayal. Ask the participants what emotions this passage brings up for them.

Brave Talk

This chapter poses three theological issues that may affect how a church
responds to people experiencing domestic abuse: submission, divorce,
and forgiveness and reconciliation. Which of these topics would you
like to discuss with other group members? Which of the three concepts
do you see at work in your own life, in your community, or in your faith
community?

Closing

Spend a few minutes processing how your local church or small group
might better respond to those experiencing domestic violence. Ask each
participant to name one takeaway they have from this chapter. Consider
making plans as a community to observe Domestic Violence Awareness
month in October.

Session 5: Let's Talk About Racism

Preparation

The racial make-up of your group, the comfort level of each individual participant, and previous experiences group members have had in talking about racism will shape how this conversation unfolds. Be brave as you begin this session, and name for the group what might be the "elephant in the room." For example, you might say, "Our group is all white." Or "We aren't as diverse as we'd like to be." Or "We know that this is an issue our faith community/neighborhood/city/state is dealing with right now because of _____." As the leader, you will set the tone for sharing honestly, showing respect to fellow group members, and holding space for participants' stories. Consider the racial history of your congregation and your town or city. For example, was your church founded because of "white flight"—that is, white people leaving cities for the suburbs? Was your town once a place where enslaved persons were brought and sold? Did race riots break out in the 1960s in your community? Gather these bits of information as facts to offer during the "Brave Talk" section.

Opening

Review the "Brave Church Covenant." Take a few moments to define the word *racism* as outlined in the "Brave Exploration" section. Allow group members to reflect on the thoughts or feelings that arise when they hear the word *racism*, on how race has shaped their experiences, or on how racism has been a part of their lives. Share with one another any concerns or fears that arise at the prospect of talking about racism.

Prayer

Ask one group member to offer this prayer: *God, your presence radiates throughout this room as we come together today. We come to make space in our hearts for new stories. Give us the courage to recognize our biases, and help*

us to let go of the prejudices that hinder our ability to see one another clearly.
Expand our vision of what it means to become a beloved community. Amen.

Reading

Read Matthew 7:1-5 aloud. Jesus asks his followers to consider the way they perceive themselves and one another. How can we examine the logs in our own eyes—that is, our blind spots and biases? In what ways have we made assumptions about others based on our perceptions of their racial identity?

Brave Talk

Consider as a group the "single stories" you've shared or believed about other races or cultures. What practical steps can you take as individuals and as a group to live into more inclusive ones? How have the events of 2020 and the growth of the Black Lives Matter movement shaped your recognition of or response to racism in your community?

Closing

Consider how this session was only just the beginning of a longer and much needed conversation about racism's role in shaping our history and everyday life. What type of further conversation about racism would your group like to have in the future?

Session 6: Let's Talk About Sexuality

Preparation

Begin by taking stock of your denomination's relationship to the LGBTQ community. What is your denomination's history, and how does it engage with LGBTQ persons now, if at all? Your denomination's background and current rules regarding church membership and leadership will shape the conversation in this session. Be mindful of your own beliefs and experiences and what you are bringing to the session. If this has been a particularly divisive topic in your faith community, ask participants to approach this conversation with an open heart and mind and willingness to listen to their neighbors' experiences before sharing their own.

Opening

Review the "Brave Church Covenant." Then, invite participants to pause and look at each person present in the session. Ask each participant to look at the person on either side of them. Then, invite them to take turns looking their neighbor in the eye and saying, "You are made in the image of God."

Prayer

Ask one group member to offer this body prayer, while everyone follows along as they are able.

God who made the heavens (reach toward the sky)
God who made the earth below (reach toward your toes)
God who made me (hands to heart)
And my neighbors near and far (stretch to the right, stretch to the left)
Help me to know that it is your light (reach toward the sky)
And it is your peace (reach toward your toes)
That ground me (hands to heart)
In this community (stretch to the right, stretch to the left)
Amen (hands folded together).

Reading

Read Genesis 1:1-27 aloud. We are made in the image of God. Not just some of us but all of us. As children of God, we share God's likeness. How might this belief shape your conversation about sexual orientation and gender identity?

Brave Talk

Describe a relationship you've built from affection (*storge*). How did this affection come to be? How has this affection kept you in a relationship despite differences or tension between you? Consider how you've stayed (or not) in relationship with those who have different views on sexuality than you. What encouragement did you gain from the two churches mentioned in this chapter?

Closing

Brainstorm with your group about a practical action you can take to show God's love to those within the LGBTQ community without any agenda.

Session 7 (Optional): Let's Keep Talking

Preparation

If you can meet in person, invite group members to someone's home for a meal or to a restaurant. If you are meeting virtually, make plans to gather online in a celebratory way. The purpose of this bonus gathering is to honor your group's willingness to practice becoming a brave church and to consider ways that you can keep the conversation going. In whatever way is possible and appropriate for your group, make the gathering fun! Set a theme, and encourage people to dress up. Play music that people can dance to. Set out festive table decorations. Wear funny hats. Do whatever will bring joy to your community.

Opening

After an informal time of being together, eating, and sharing, ask the participants to consider these questions: How have I changed over the course of this study? What did I learn that I did not know before? How have my relationships with the people in this group changed?

Prayer

Ask one group member to offer this prayer: *God, none of us could have imagined where this journey of faith would take us. As these sessions come to an end, we give thanks to you, Surprising One. For the gift of seeing anew our traveling companions. For moments of connection. For the experience of listening and then listening some more to people we don't always understand. For fresh perspectives and insights. For unlikely friendships. God, you have brought forth new things in us. We've asked new questions of ourselves and of our church. As we look to what might be ahead, we thank you for already preparing a way. Amen.*

Reading

Read Acts 10:1-35 aloud. Where are the winds of the Spirit blowing in your group or faith community? How have you seen God at work among you?

Brave Talk

Review "Resources for Further Study and Conversation," which begins on page 139. What books, organizations, or articles are you already familiar with? Which would you like to read or learn more about? What other materials not listed might you recommend to others? Discuss how you would like to continue your brave conversations in the future.

Closing

Invite group members to offer their response to this thanksgiving prayer for your time together. Have every member share a response to the following: "We thank God for _____."

APPENDIX A

Brave Church Covenant

We, the members of _____ (group name), commit to talking about real life together as we tackle the tough topics in this study, beginning _____ (date) and concluding _____ (date). We realize that entering into these conversations can bring up painful experiences as well as sources of conflict. We make the following promises to one another:

1. We will accept conflict and commit to the way of kindness.
2. We will take responsibility for how our own words are received.
3. We will ask permission before we challenge someone's views on a subject.
4. We will show respect for one another and graciously receive feedback if someone feels disrespected.
5. We will use "I" statements instead of "you" statements. We will not accuse or attack.

We covenant to make this time holy and to hold in confidence all that is shared within this group.

_____   _____

_____   _____

APPENDIX B

A Prayer for Mother's Day

Today we celebrate mothers.
Thank God for mothers!
For the women who have joined God in heaven and whom we miss dearly here on earth
For the mothers of the past, we thank God.
For the women who are raising and making sacrifices for their children
For the mothers of today, we thank God.
For the women who have taken in children through foster care and adoption and who show us that a mother's love extends beyond biological ties
For the mothers with big hearts, we thank God.
For the women who have lost a child to death or want a child they know they can't have
For the mothers who are so strong, we thank God.
For the women who are "mother hens" in our community and who nurture, support, and guide us
For the mothers in spirit, we thank God.
For the women who raised us in hurtful ways but whose lives spur us toward healthier paths
For the mothers who pushed us on our way, we thank God.
For God, whose love remains a constant source of comfort in all of our lives

For the comfort of your constant love, God, we thank you.
We thank you, God, for your steadfast love and for the women whose love has shaped our lives in so many ways. Help us to honor them in everything we do.
Amen.

A Prayer for Father's Day

Today we celebrate fathers!
Thank God for fathers!
For the men who have left this earth and whom we dearly miss
For the fathers of the past whose legacy remains strong, we thank God.
For the men who are raising and making sacrifices for their children
For the fathers of today, we thank God.
For the men who have taken in children through foster care and adoption and who show us that a father's love extends beyond biological ties
For the fathers with big hearts, we thank God.
For the men who have lost a child to death or who want a child they know they can't have
For the fathers who carry heavy burdens, we thank God.
For the men in our community who model for us the fruits of the Spirit— love, joy, peace, patience, kindness, goodness, and faithfulness
For the fathers in spirit, we thank God.
For the father who raised us in hurtful ways but whose lives spur us toward healthier paths
For the fathers who pushed us on our way, we thank God.
For God, Our Father, whose unconditional love remains constant in all of our lives
For your steadfast love, God, we thank you.
We thank you, God, for the men who have influenced our lives in so many ways. We lift our voices in your name, O Heavenly Father, whom we adore.
Amen.

NOTES

Introduction

1. Rachel G. Hackenberg, "Secrets Too Deep for Words," in *Denial is My Spiritual Practice: (And Other Failures of Faith)*, by Rachel G. Hackenberg and Martha Spong (New York: Church Publishing, 2018), 58–59.
2. Elizabeth Hagan, *Birthed: Finding Grace Through Infertility* (St. Louis, MO: Chalice Press, 2016).
3. Henri J. M. Nouwen, *Love, Henri: Letters on the Spiritual Life* (New York: Convergent Books, 2016), 251.

Chapter 1: Let's Talk

1. Adapted from Justin McRoberts and Scott Erickson, Prayer 2 and Prayer 13, *Prayer: Forty Days of Practice* (New York: WaterBrook, 2019).
2. Diana Ali, "Safe Spaces and Brave Spaces: Historical Context and Recommendations for Student Affairs Professionals," *National Association of Student Professional Administrators Policy and Practice Series*, no. 1 (October 2017), 4-6, http://www.naspa.org/images/uploads/main/Policy_and_Practice_No_2_Safe_Brave_Spaces.pdf.
3. Brian Arao and Kristi Clemens, "From Safe Spaces to Brave Spaces: A New Way to Frame Dialogue around Diversity and Social Justice," *The Art of Effective Facilitation: Reflections from Social Justice*

Educators, ed. Lisa M. Landreman (Sterling, VA: Stylus Publishing, 2013), 139.

4. Arao and Clemens, "From Safe Spaces to Brave Spaces," 136–49.
5. Carrie Zimmerman, in conversation with the author, June 2019.
6. Arao and Clemens, "From Safe Spaces to Brave Spaces," 143–44.
7. Arao and Clemens, "From Safe Spaces to Brave Spaces," 144–46.
8. Brené Brown, *Braving the Wilderness: The Quest for True Belonging and the Courage to Stand Alone* (New York: Random House, 2017), 69.
9. Barbara Brown Taylor, *An Altar in the World: A Geography of Faith* (New York: HarperOne, 2009), 114.
10. Arao and Clemens, "From Safe Spaces to Brave Spaces," 147–48.
11. Arao and Clemens, "From Safe Spaces to Brave Spaces," 148.

Chapter 2: Let's Talk About Infertility and Miscarriage

1. "Infertility FAQ," RESOLVE: The National Infertility Association, accessed September 2020, https://resolve.org/infertility-101 /infertility-faq/. The website explains that infertility is "diagnosed after a couple has had one year of unprotected, well-timed intercourse, or if the woman has suffered from multiple miscarriages and the woman is under thirty-five years of age. If the woman is over thirty-five years old, it is diagnosed after six months of unprotected, well-timed intercourse."
2. "Pregnancy Loss," Office on Women's Health, United States Department of Health and Human Services, https://www.womenshealth .gov/pregnancy/youre-pregnant-now-what/pregnancy-loss.
3. "Infertility FAQ," RESOLVE.
4. Bethany L. Johnson and Margaret M. Quinlan, *You're Doing It Wrong: Mothering, Media, and Medical Expertise* (New Brunswick, NJ: Rutgers University Press, 2019), 33.
5. Elizabeth Hagan, *Birthed: Finding Grace Through Infertility* (St. Louis, MO: Chalice Press, 2016).
6. Cherry White, in conversation with the author, July 2019.
7. Oliva B. Waxman, "The Surprisingly Sad Origins of Mother's Day," *Time*, May 11, 2017, https://time.com/4771354/mothers-day -history-origins/.

8. Kristine Phillips, "The Woman Who Invented Mother's Day Would Absolutely Hate What It Is Today," *The Washington Post,* May 14, 2017, https://www.washingtonpost.com/news/retropolis/wp/2017/05/14/the-woman-who-invented-mothers-day-would-absolutely-hate-what-it-is-today/.

9. "Methodist History: First Father's Day at Church," The United Methodist Church, June 13, 2015, http://www.umc.org/who-we-are/methodist-history-first-fathers-day-at-church. The Central United Methodist Church was then called Williams Memorial Methodist Episcopal Church.

10. Olivia Waxman, "How the Radical '60s and '70s Helped Make Father's Day a National Holiday," *Time*, June 16, 2017, https://time.com/4811771/fathers-day-origins-history/.

11. "About," Moms in the Making, accessed September 2020, http://momsinthemakinggroup.com/about/.

12. Alexia Fernandez, "Five Myths About Women of Color, Infertility and IVF Debunked," *The Atlantic*, September 3, 2015, https://www.theatlantic.com/politics/archive/2015/09/five-myths-about-women-of-color-infertility-and-ivf-debunked/432711/.

13. Stacey Edwards-Dunn, "How One Woman's Road to Pregnancy Led Her to Confront Stereotypes About Black Woman and Fertility," interview by Piya Chattopadhyay, *Out in the Open*, CBC radio, January 3, 2020.

14. "About Us," Fertility for Colored Girls, accessed March 2020, https://www.fertilityforcoloredgirls.org/about_us.

15. Sarah Sisson Rollandini, in conversation with the author, July 2019.

16. For more information, see "Orphan Sunday," Christian Alliance for Orphans, accessed September 2020, https://www.cafo.org/orphansunday/about.

Chapter 3: Let's Talk About Mental Illness

1. "Learn About Mental Health," Centers for Disease Control and Prevention, updated January 2018, https://www.cdc.gov/mentalhealth/learn/index.htm.

2. "Mental Health Information," National Institute of Mental Health," accessed September 2020, https://www.nimh.nih.gov/health/statistics/mental-illness.shtml.

3. "Mental Health Information," NIMH.

4. "Learn About Mental Health," CDC.

5. "Learn About Mental Health," CDC.

6. Amy Simpson, *Troubled Minds: Mental Illness and the Church's Mission* (Downers Grove, IL: InterVarsity Press, 2013), 53.

7. LifeWay Research, *Study of Acute Mental Illness and Christian Faith: Research Report*, 2014, http://lifewayresearch.com/wp-content/uploads/2014/09/Acute-Mental-Illness-and-Christian-Faith-Research-Report-1.pdf.

8. LifeWay Research, *Study of Acute Mental Illness.*

9. "Mental Health Myths and Facts," MentalHealth.gov, updated August 2017, https://www.mentalhealth.gov/basics/mental-health-myths-facts.

10. "Language Matters in Mental Health," Hogg Foundation for Mental Health, accessed September 2020, https://hogg.utexas.edu/news-resources/publications/language-matters-in-mental-health.

11. Brené Brown, *Daring Greatly: How the Courage to Be Vulnerable Transforms the Way We Live, Love, Parent, and Lead* (New York: Gotham Books, 2015), 34.

12. Brown, *Daring Greatly*, 34.

13. Ed Stetzer, "The Church and Mental Health: What Do the Numbers Tell Us?" *Christianity Today*, April 20, 2018, https://www.christianitytoday.com/edstetzer/2018/april/church-and-mental-health.html.

14. Alyssa Newcomb, "Pastor Rick Warren's Son Matthew Commits Suicide After Lifelong Battle with Mental Illness," ABC News, April 6, 2013, https://abcnews.go.com/US/pastor-rick-warrens-son-matthew-commits-suicide-lifelong/story?id=18897249.

15. Rick Warren and Kay Warren, "Rick Warren: Churches Must Do More to Address Mental Illness," *Time*, March 27, 2014, https://time.com/40071/rick-warren-churches-must-do-more-to-address-mental-illness/.

16. "Homelessness and Mental Illness: A Challenge to Our Society," Brain & Behavior Research Foundation, November 19, 2018, https://www.bbrfoundation.org/blog/homelessness-and-mental -illness-challenge-our-society.

17. Simpson, *Troubled Minds,* 99.

18. Simpson, *Troubled Minds,* 98.

19. Tyler Sit, in conversation with the author, July 2019.

20. "Resources," New City Church, Minneapolis, MN, accessed March 2020, http://grownewcity.church/resources.

21. Sit, July 2019.

22. "Our History," Christ Church, Charlotte, NC, accessed March 2020, http://www.christchurchcharlotte.org/about/our-history/.

23. Chip Evans, quoted in Ken Garfield, "A Church Invests in Mental Health in Response to Parishioners' Suffering," *Faith & Leadership*, July 9, 2019, https://www.faithandleadership.com/church-invests -mental-health-response-parishioners-suffering.

24. Jon Kocmond, quoted in Garfield, "A Church Invests in Mental Health."

25. Christ Church, "Welcome Our New Wellness Director," news release, August 29, 2019, http://www.christchurchcharlotte.org/article/welcome -our-new-wellness-director/#.

Chapter 4: Let's Talk About Domestic Violence

1. J. Clinton McCann, Jr., "Book of Psalms," in Leander E. Keck et al., eds., *The New Interpreter's Bible*, vol. IV (Nashville, TN: Abingdon, 1996), 898.

2. All the names in this chapter have been changed for protection.

3. "Preventing Intimate Partner Violence," Centers for Disease Control and Prevention, accessed September 2020, https://www.cdc.gov /violenceprevention/intimatepartnerviolence/fastfact.html.

4. "Preventing Intimate Partner Violence," CDC.

5. "Preventing Intimate Partner Violence," CDC.

6. "Understand Relationship Abuse," National Domestic Violence Hotline, accessed September 2020, https://www.thehotline.org /identify-abuse/understand-relationship-abuse/.

7. Rachel G. Hackenberg, "Secrets Too Deep for Words," in *Denial is My Spiritual Practice: (And Other Failures of Faith)*, by Rachel G. Hackenberg and Martha Spong (New York: Church Publishing, 2018), 60.

8. Patricia Tjaden and Nancy Thoennes, "Extent, Nature, and Consequences of Intimate Partner Violence: Findings from the National Violence Against Women Survey," United States Department of Justice, July 2000, https://www.ncjrs.gov/pdffiles1/nij/181867.pdf.

9. LifeWay Research, *Domestic Violence and the Church: Research Report*, sponsored by Autumn Miles, 2016, http://lifewayresearch.com/wp-content/uploads/2017/02/Domestic-Violence-and-the-Church-Research-Report.pdf.

10. LifeWay Research, *Domestic Violence*.

11. Bob Smietana, "How Pastors Perceive Domestic Violence Differently," *Christianity Today*, February 20, 2017, https://www.christianitytoday.com/news/2017/february/how-pastors-perceive-domestic-violence-lifeway-autumn-miles.html.

12. Natalie Hoffman, "Christians Say the Darndest Things," *Flying Free* (blog), May 7, 2019, https://flyingfreenow.com/christians-say-the-darndest-things-a-series-of-unfortunate-cliches-01/.

13. Hoffman, "Christians Say the Darndest Things."

14. Southern Baptist Convention, *The Baptist Faith and Message 2000*, accessed September 2020, http://www.sbc.net/bfm2000/bfm2000.asp.

15. Paige Patterson, "Advice to Victims of Domestic Violence," 2000, Internet Archive, audio recording, https://archive.org/details/PaigePattersonsbcAdviceToVictimsOfDomesticViolence.

16. Patterson, "Advice to Victims."

17. Michael Gryboski, "Paige Patterson to Step Down as President of Seminary Following Spousal Abuse Comments," *The Christian Post*, May 23, 2018, https://www.christianpost.com/news/paige-patterson-to-step-down-as-president-of-seminary-following-spousal-abuse-comments.html.

18. Leslie Copeland-Tune, "Hot Grits Are Good For Women," *Mondays at the Altar* (blog), August 14, 2015, https://mondaysatthealtar.com/2015/08/14/hot-grits-are-good-for-eating/.

19. Beth Moore (@BethMooreLPM), Twitter, April 28, 2018, https://twitter.com/BethMooreLPM/status/990417498607468544.

20. Autumn Miles, "The NFL and the Church Share a Culture of Silence on Abuse," guest post, *The Christian Century*, September 19, 2014, https://www.christiancentury.org/blogs/archive/2014-09/nfl-and-church-share-culture-silence-abuse.

21. Autumn Miles, "How Southern Baptist Leaders Aided My Escape from Abuse," *Christianity Today*, May 18, 2019, https://www.christianitytoday.com/ct/2018/may-web-only/paige-patterson-southern-baptist-leaders-aided-escape-abuse.html.

22. Brenda Branson and Paula J. Silva, *Violence Among Us: Ministry to Families in Crisis* (Valley Forge, PA: Judson Press, 2007), 82.

23. Suzanne Degges-White, "Intimate Partner Violence: Walk Away Before the Cycle Starts," *Psychology Today*, February 27, 2015, https://www.psychologytoday.com/us/blog/lifetime-connections/201502/intimate-partner-abuse-walk-away-the-cycle-starts.

24. Julie Owens, quoted in Smietana, "How Pastors Perceive Domestic Violence."

25. Owens, quoted in Smietana, "How Pastors Perceive Domestic Violence."

26. "Should I Go to Couple's Therapy with my Abusive Partner?" National Domestic Violence Hotline, accessed September 2020, https://www.thehotline.org/resources/should-i-go-to-couples-therapy-with-my-abusive-partner/.

27. Christy Gunter Sim, *Survivor Care: What Religious Professionals Need to Know About Healing Trauma* (Nashville, TN: General Board of Higher Education and Ministry, The United Methodist Church, 2019), 163.

28. Lesley-Ann Hix Tommey, in conversation with the author, September 2019.

29. "History," Metro Baptist Church, accessed March 20020, http://mbcnyc.org/about/history-and-building.

30. "Living Well Life Skills Empowerment Program," Rauschenbusch Metro Ministries, accessed March 2020, http://www.rmmnyc.org /programs/living-well.
31. Tommey, September 2019.
32. "New York Church Expands Programs for Young Adults," Disciples of Christ, April 4, 2018, https://disciples.org/congregations/new -york-church-expands-programs-for-young-adults/.
33. Stephanie Kendell, in conversation with the author, September 2019.
34. One example is Judges 19. For suggestions on how to teach or preach this passage, see Sarah Jobe, "Giving Voice to the Voiceless: Preaching Judges 19," *Working Preacher*, Luther Seminary, July 12, 2010, https://www.workingpreacher.org/craft.aspx?post=1876.
35. Kendell, September 2019.

Chapter 5: Let's Talk About Racism

1. *Merriam-Webster*, s.v. "racism," accessed September 20, 2020, https://www.merriam-webster.com/dictionary/racism.
2. *Merriam-Webster*, s.v. "racism."
3. David Morgan and Richard Cowan, "George Floyd's Brother Decries a 'Modern-Day Lynching' in Testimony to Congress," *Reuters*, June 10, 2020, https://www.reuters.com/article/us-minneapolis-police -protests/george-floyds-brother-decries-a-modern-day-lynching-in -testimony-to-congress-idUSKBN23H1NB.
4. Chimamanda Ngozi Adichie, "The Danger of a Single Story," filmed 2009, TEDGlobal video, 18:14, https://www.ted.com/talks /chimamanda_adichie_the_danger_of_a_single_story.
5. Adichie, "The Danger of a Single Story."
6. Ta-Nehisi Coates, "Letter to My Son," *The Atlantic*, July 4, 2015, https://www.theatlantic.com/politics/archive/2015/07/tanehisi -coates-between-the-world-and-me/397619/.
7. Austin Channing Brown, *I'm Still Here: Black Dignity in a World Made for Whiteness* (Nashville, TN: Convergent Books, 2018), 22–23.
8. Abby Hailey, email message to the author, February 2019.

9. Hailey, February 2019.
10. Hailey, email message to the author, September 2020.
11. Hailey, February 2019.
12. "About," Martin Luther King, Jr. Christian Church, accessed March 2020, http://mlkchristianchurch.org/about/.
13. Jean Robinson-Casey, in conversation with the author, February 2019.
14. Robinson-Casey, February 2019.
15. Robinson-Casey, February 2019.
16. Robinson-Casey, in conversation with the author, September 2020.
17. Robinson-Casey, September 2020.

Chapter 6: Let's Talk About Sexuality

1. Commentators help us to understand the word *image* refers to "the entire human being, not some part, as the reason or the will." Terence E. Fretheim, "The Book of Genesis," in Leander E. Keck et al., eds., *The New Interpreter's Bible*, vol. I (Nashville, TN: Abingdon, 1994), 345.
2. Kara Fox, Henrik Pettersson, and Eliza Mackintosh, "Where Being Gay Is Illegal Around the World," CNN, April 8, 2019, https://www.cnn.com/2019/04/03/world/same-sex-laws-map-intl/index.html.
3. David Masci, Anna Brown, and Jocelyn Kiley, "Five Facts About Same-Sex Marriage," *Fact Tank: News in the Numbers*, Pew Research Center, Washington DC, June 24, 2019, https://www.pewresearch.org/fact-tank/2019/06/24/same-sex-marriage/.
4. Masci, Brown, and Kiley, "Five Facts About Same-Sex Marriage."
5. Masci, Brown, and Kiley, "Five Facts About Same-Sex Marriage."
6. William B. Lawrence, quoted in Emily McFarlan Miller, "Why Is Sexuality Such a Big Deal for the Church?" *Religious News Service*, August 22, 2017, https://religionnews.com/2017/08/22/why-is-sexuality-such-a-big-deal-for-the-church/.
7. David Masci and Michael Lipka, "Where Christian Churches, Other Religions Stand on Gay Marriage," *Fact Tank: News in the Numbers*, Pew Research Center, Washington DC, December 21,

2015, https://www.pewresearch.org/fact-tank/2015/12/21/where-christian-churches-stand-on-gay-marriage/.

8. Emily McFarlan Miller, "United Methodists Reschedule Meeting—and Decision on Splitting—to 2021," *Religious News Service*, May 27, 2020, https://religionnews.com/2020/05/27/united-methodist-reschedule-meeting-and-decision-on-splitting-to-2021/.

9. Celeste Gracey and Jeremy Weber, "World Vision Reverses Decision to Hire Christians in Same-Sex Marriages," *Christianity Today*, March 26, 2014, https://www.christianitytoday.com/ct/2014/march-web-only/world-vision-reverses-decision-gay-same-sex-marriage.html.

10. C. S. Lewis, *The Four Loves* (New York: Harcourt Brace, 1960), 33.

11. Lewis, *The Four Loves*, 36.

12. Scott Bader-Saye, "Bonds of Affection: How Do We Love When We Disagree?" *The Christian Century*, November 11, 2014, https://www.christiancentury.org/article/2014-11/bonds-affection.

13. Bader-Saye, "Bonds of Affection."

14. Matthew Vines, *God and the Gay Christian: The Biblical Case in Support of Same-Sex Relationships* (New York: Convergent, 2014), 8.

15. "A Survey of LGBT Americans," Pew Research Center, Washington, DC, June 13, 3013, https://www.pewsocialtrends.org/2013/06/13/a-survey-of-lgbt-americans/.

16. Preston Sprinkle, *People to Be Loved: Why Homosexuality Is Not Just an Issue* (Grand Rapids, MI: Zondervan, 2015), 14.

17. Vines, *God and the Gay Christian*, 9.

18. "History," Baptist Church of the Covenant, accessed September 2020, https://www.bcoc.net/history.

19. Sarah Jackson Shelton, in conversation with author, August 8, 2019.

20. Shelton, August 2019.

21. Mike Casey, member of BCOC's Council on Mission, email message to the author, August 13, 2019.

22. Carol Cannon, "St. Andrew's Completes a Successful Study on Human Sexuality and the UMC," *South Carolina United Methodist Advocate*, May 25, 2018, https://www.advocatesc.org/2018/05/st-andrews-completes-successful-study-on-human-sexuality-and-the-umc/.

23. For an example, see: "Soul Supper at Highland Baptist Church Provides Safe Space for LGBT Community," WHAS 11, ABC video, Louisville, KY: WHAS, November, 10, 2018, https://www.whas11.com/video/life/heartwarming/soul-supper-at-highland-baptist-church-provides-safe-space-for-lgbt-community/417-8309564.

Chapter 7: Let's Keep Talking

1. Vaughan S. Roberts and David Sims, *Leading by Story: Rethinking Church Leadership* (London: SCM Press, 2017), 79.
2. Amy Butler, "I Preached About a Gun Rights Advocate. He Wasn't Who I Thought," June 23, 2017, https://www.usatoday.com/story/opinion/2017/06/23/liberal-pastor-conservative-gun-activist-we-have-to-keep-talking-amy-butler-column/103007558/.
3. "Our Story: Building a House United," Braver Angels, accessed March 2020, https://www.better-angels.org/what-we-do/.
4. Scott Ramsey, in conversation with the author, July 27, 2019.
5. Ramsey, July 2019.
6. "Our Story," Braver Angels.
7. Ramsey, July 2019.
8. Mel Pine, email message to the author, August 24, 2019.
9. Jan Mercker, "Bursting Bubbles: Local Group Works to Bridge the Red-Blue Divide," Loudon Now, October 4, 2018, https://loudounnow.com/2018/10/04/bursting-bubbles-local-group-works-to-bridge-the-red-blue-divide.
10. Pine, August 2019.
11. Rebecca Anderson, quoted in Celeste Kennel-Shank, "At Gilead Church Chicago, Storytelling Is Central to Worship," *The Christian Century*, April 9, 2019, https://www.christiancentury.org/article/features/gilead-church-chicago-storytelling-central-worship.
12. Vince Amlin, in conversation with the author, August 27, 2019.
13. Amlin, 2019.
14. Kennel-Shank, "At Gilead Church Chicago."
15. "TODAY Visits the Church that Holds Its Services in a Pub," video, NBC, April 11, 2017, https://www.today.com/video/today-visits-the-church-that-holds-its-services-in-a-pub-918603331630.

RESOURCES FOR FURTHER STUDY AND CONVERSATION

Chapter 1: Let's Talk

Brown, Brené. *Braving the Wilderness: The Quest for True Belonging and the Courage to Stand Alone.* New York: Random House, 2017.

"Dialogue and Exchange." Hosted by Guy Raz. *TED Radio Hour.* Podcast audio. National Public Radio, October 27, 2017. https://www.npr.org/programs/ted-radio-hour/558307433.

Markman, Art. "Agreeing to Disagree: The Difference Between Talking at and Talking with Someone Else." *Psychology Today,* June 17, 2010. https://www.psychologytoday.com/us/blog/ulterior-motives/201006/agreeing-disagree-the-difference-between-talking-and-talking-someone.

Patterson, Kerry, Joseph Grenny, Ron McMillan, and Al Switzer. *Crucial Conversations: Tools for Talking When Stakes Are High.* New York: McGraw-Hill, 2012.

Chapter 2: Let's Talk About Infertility and Miscarriage

Barrett, Elise Erikson. *What Was Lost: A Christian Journey through Miscarriage.* Louisville, KY: Westminster John Knox, 2010.

Catholic Infertility Ministry. https://www.catholicinfertilityministry.com/.

Freedman, Joy M. and Tabatha D. Johnson, eds. *Still a Mother: Journey through Perinatal Bereavement*. Valley Forge, PA: Judson Press, 2016.

Hanchey, Mary Elizabeth Hill and Erin K. McClain, eds. *Through the Darkness Gather Round: Devotions About Infertility, Miscarriage, and Infant Loss*. Macon, GA: Smyth and Helwys, 2015.

Mullins, Brandy H. and Tiffney Patterson *Out of the Depths: Your Companion After Pregnancy or Infant Loss*. Nashville, TN: Abingdon Press, 2019.

Newton, Lisa. *Amateur Nester: Christian Encouragement During Infertility* (blog). https://www.amateurnester.com/.

Chapter 3: Let's Talk About Mental Health

Coleman, Monica A. *Bipolar Faith: A Black Woman's Journey with Depression and Faith*. Minneapolis, MN: Fortress Press, 2016.

"Congregational Toolkits." United Church of Christ Mental Health Network. https://www.mhn-ucc.org/congregational-toolkits/.

Grcevich, Stephen. *Mental Health and the Church: A Ministry Handbook for Including Children and Adults with ADHD, Anxiety, Mood Disorders, and Other Common Mental Health Conditions*. Grand Rapids, MI: Zondervan, 2018.

Interfaith Network on Mental Illness. http://inmi.us/.

Mental Health First Aid. https://www.mentalhealthfirstaid.org/.

Mental Health Ministries. http://www.mentalhealthministries.net/.

"Minority Mental Health Month Resources." National Alliance on Mental Illness. https://www.nami.org/Get-Involved/Awareness-Events/Minority-Mental-Health-Awareness-Month.

Stanford, Matthew S. *Grace for the Afflicted: A Clinical and Biblical Perspective on Mental Illness*. Downers Grove, IL: InterVarsity Press, 2017.

Chapter 4: Let's Talk About Domestic Violence

Burton, Susan. "Articulating our Theology: Domestic Violence." Webinar. The United Methodist Church. https://www.youtube.com/watch?v=d-BJNugdQqo.

Document the Abuse. http://documenttheabuse.com/.

"Domestic Violence." United Church of Christ. https://www.ucc.org/justice_womens-issues_domestic-violence.

"Domestic Violence Awareness." United Methodist Women. https://www.unitedmethodistwomen.org/domestic-violence.

Faith Trust Institute. https://faithtrustinstitute.org.

FOCUS Ministries. https://www.focusministries1.org/.

"Gender-Based Violence." Evangelical Lutheran Church in America. https://www.elca.org/Faith/Faith-and-Society/Social-Messages/Gender-Violence.

Sim, Christy Gunter. *Survivor Care: What Religious Professionals Need to Know About Healing Trauma.* Nashville, TN: General Board of Higher Education and Ministry, The United Methodist Church, 2017.

Trible, Phyllis. *Texts of Terror: Literary-Feminist Readings of Biblical Narratives.* Minneapolis, MN: Fortress Press, 1984.

Chapter 5: Let's Talk About Racism

"Anti-Racism Resources." United Church of Christ. https://www.ucc.org/justice_advocacy_resources_pdfs_anti-racism_anti-racism-resources.

Challenging Racism. http://www.challengingracism.org/.

Coates, Ta-Nehisi. *Between the World and Me.* New York: Spiegel & Grau, 2015.

DiAngelo, Robin. *White Fragility: Why It's So Hard for White People to Talk About Racism.* Boston: Beacon Press, 2018.

"Facing Racism: A Vision of Intercultural Community Antiracism Study Guides." Presbyterian Church (USA). https://www.presbyterian mission.org/resource/facing-racism-vision-intercultural -community-antiracism-study-guides/.

Helsel, Carolyn B. *Anxious to Talk About It: Helping White Christians Talk Faithfully About Racism.* St. Louis, MO: Chalice Press, 2017.

Kendi, Ibram X. *How to Be an Antiracist.* New York: One World, 2019.

Repairs of the Breach. https://www.breachrepairers.org.

Tatum, Beverly Daniel. *Why Are All the Black Kids Sitting Together in the Cafeteria? And Other Conversation about Race.* New York: Basic Books, 1997.

White Ally Toolkit. https://www.whiteallytoolkit.com/.

Chapter 6: Let's Talk About Sexuality

Choplin, Leslie and Jenny Beaumont. *These Are Our Bodies: Talking Faith & Sexuality at Church & Home.* Atlanta, GA: Church Publishing, 2016.

Chu, Jeff. *Does Jesus Really Love Me? A Gay Christian's Pilgrimage in Search of God in America.* New York: Harper Perennial, 2013.

Cottrell, Susan. *Mom, I'm Gay: Loving Your LBGTQ Child and Strengthening Your Faith.* Louisville, KY: Westminster John Knox, 2016.

For the Bible Tells Me So. Film. http://www.forthebibletellsmeso.org/.

Kim-Kort, Mihee. *Outside the Lines: How Embracing Queerness Will Transform Your Faith.* Minneapolis, MN: Fortress Press, 2018.

McCleneghan, Bromleigh. *Good Christian Sex: Why Chastity Isn't the Only Option—And Other Things the Bible Says About Sex.* San Francisco: HarperOne, 2016.

Our Whole Lives. Education programs. United Church of Christ. https://www.ucc.org/justice_sexuality-education_our-whole-lives.

"Sexuality Education." Religious Institute. http://religiousinstitute.org /issue/sexuality-education/.

Chapter 7: Let's Keep Talking

Brown, Brené. *Dare to Lead: Brave Work. Tough Conversations. Whole Hearts.* New York: Random House, 2018.

Denker, Angela. *Red State Christians: Understanding the Voters Who Elected Donald Trump.* Minneapolis, MN: Fortress Press, 2019.

Faith Rooted Storytelling and Public Narrative. Workshop. Auburn Seminary. https://auburnseminary.org/storytelling-public-narrative/.

Gladwell, Malcolm. *Talking to Strangers: What We Should Know About People We Don't Know.* New York: Little, Brown and Company, 2019.

Our Community Listens. Workshops. https://www.ourcommunity listens.org/.

Parker, Palmer. "The Circle of Trust Approach." Center for Courage & Renewal. http://www.couragerenewal.org/approach/.

Story Corps. https://storycorps.org/stories/.

Williams, Layton E. *Holy Disunity: How What Separates Us Can Save Us.* Louisville, KY: Westminster John Knox, 2019.